UNIVERSITY OF NORTH CAROLINA
STUDIES IN THE ROMANCE LANGUAGES AND LITERATURES

Number 123

STRUCTURE AND IDEOLOGY IN BOIARDO'S
ORLANDO INNAMORATO

STRUCTURE AND IDEOLOGY IN BOIARDO'S
ORLANDO INNAMORATO

BY
ANDREA DI TOMMASO

CHAPEL HILL
THE UNIVERSITY OF NORTH CAROLINA PRESS

DEPÓSITO LEGAL: V. 3.355 - 1972

ARTES GRÁFICAS SOLER, S. A. - JÁVEA, 28 - VALENCIA (8) - 1972

Dedicated, in gratitude, to
Nathan Edelman and John Freccero

PREFACE

This study is intended as an examination of the formal and ideological structures of the *Orlando innamorato* and as an analysis of the values promoted within that poetic microcosm. It is primarily an interpretation of the fictive mode and not of the historical reality in which the fictional life of the Poem was created. The references to historical reality, therefore, are offered principally as suggestions of a possible equivalence between the values of Orlando's world and those of Boiardo's world. A lack of historical information on Ferrara prevents a literary interpreter from doing more than inferring possible correspondences between the two worlds, except where the ties are obvious. Thus, while the fact, for example, that Boiardo was an established member of nobility, who always used his title of Count (while Ariosto almost never did), appears to be relevant to the ideological structuration of the fictional world, it is not as easy to affirm that the aspirations, behavior and ethics of the fictional heroes are a reflection of the real world. Some of the suggestions, however, are too tempting to be ignored.

My thanks are due and cordially extended to Eduardo Saccone for his encouragement and many comments. I would also like to express my appreciation to my colleague, Peter Bondanella, for reading the manuscript and sharing his views with me.

A. D. T.

Detroit, Michigan
October, 1971

TABLE OF CONTENTS

	Pages
INTRODUCTION	13
CHAPTER ONE: THE POET AND HIS AUDIENCE	17
— Two: INFLAMMATION OF THE HEART	45
— THREE: THE MEANING OF NOBILITY	71
— FOUR: TIME, SPACE AND ACTION	89
BIBLIOGRAPHY	98

INTRODUCTION

In addition to the enthusiastic response received from the Este Court during the author's lifetime, the early success of the *Orlando innamorato* is marked by a series of imitations, continuations, revisions, and new editions which continued until the middle of the sixteenth century.[1] The reputation of Boiardo's Poem, however, was critically injured by the success of one of the "continuations," Ariosto's *Orlando furioso*. In the age of Pietro Bembo, which nurtured the polemic over the relative merits of invention and eloquence, Ariosto's Poem, which combined Boiardo's inventiveness with Poliziano's elegance, was far more favorably received than Boiardo's. It was the "ibridismo della lingua e le scabrosità dello stile"[2] in the *Innamorato* which led Francesco Berni and Lodovico Domenichi to rewrite Boiardo's original. These rewritings (*rifacimenti*) followed the *Orlando furioso* like a *coup de grâce*. After the middle of the *Cinquecento* Boiardo's creation was remembered only in the versions of Berni and Domenichi. The *rifacimenti*, which sought to improve the Poem by replacing Boiardo's coarse Emilian language with Tuscan elegance, received numerous editions and little opposition. The original was not reprinted again until 1830, when Antonio Panizzi, an Italian political exile living in London, published a combined edition of the *Innamorato* and the *Furioso*.

---

[1] For a comprehensive discussion of Boiardo criticism through 1959 see Giovanni Ponte, "Matteo Maria Boiardo," in *I classici italiani nella storia della critica*, ed. Walter Binni (Florence, 1965), Vol. I, pp. 269-298. The cursory remarks in this introduction are based in large part on Ponte's article, which contains all the bibliographical references to the critics mentioned herein.
[2] Vittorio Rossi, *Il Quattrocento* (Milan, 1933), p. 465.

The second half of the sixteenth century, which was less intimidated by Horace's proscription in the *Ars Poetica* against fantastic inventions, was willing to assign a higher value to inventiveness. As a consequence, Boiardo, rather than simply being condemned for lack of eloquence, received some praise for his inventiveness. The praise, however, was only indirect, for the judgments from which it emanated "erano indice non tanto di una miglior comprensione dell'*Innamorato* boiardesco, quanto di atteggiamenti polemici verso l'Ariosto." [3] Since that time all critics have agreed that Boiardo did have the power to invent. A near exception was Francesco De Sanctis, who, while he did allow that Boiardo was superior to Luigi Pulci in inventive ability, declared that invention is the least important element in art. What Boiardo lacked, according to De Sanctis, was "lo spirito e... quell'alta immaginazione artistica che si chiama fantasia." [4]

In the seventeenth century the *Orlando innamorato* received almost no attention, except for that of a few "eruditi ferraresi e reggiani" toward the end of the century. [5] The eighteenth century showed an increased attention to Boiardo, but primarily, it seems, as a sounding board for its own tastes rather than as the object of genuine critical judgments. Thus while Gravina and Conti praised Boiardo for his moderate "classicismo", Baretti later admired his spontaneous "espressione individuale." [6]

By the beginning of the Romantic era the traditional view of Boiardo had become that of the inventive poet who lacked dignity of style. The critics of the early nineteenth century sought to find new reasons for appreciating the *Orlando innamorato*. Ugo Foscolo in his discourse *Sui poemi narrativi e romanzeschi italiani* suggested that Boiardo's genius was most evident in his ability to "disegnare i caratteri". [7] Friedrich Schlegel, while again noting Ariosto's superior facility with language, suggested that Boiardo was superior to Ariosto because he dealt with chivalry seriously

---

[3] Ponte, p. 270.
[4] Francesco De Sanctis, "Storia della letteratura italiana," in *Opere*, ed. Niccolò Gallo (Milan, 1961), pp. 369-70.
[5] Ponte, p. 271.
[6] *Ibid.*, p. 273.
[7] Ugo Foscolo, *Opere edite e postume*, Vol. X: *Saggi di critica storico-letteraria* (Florence, 1859), p. 179.

rather than ironically. Later De Sanctis was to offer the contrary opinion that Boiardo's Poem was a failure precisely because he tried to deal seriously with a subject which could no longer be taken seriously. In his essay *La poesia cavalleresca* he said: "Ricapitolandoci sul Boiardo diremo che i suoi difetti consistono in un fondo ridicolo trattato con l'apparenza della serietà". [8] De Sanctis does say, however, as did Foscolo, that Boiardo "è uno de' principali disegnatori della poesia italiana." [9] After De Sanctis' unsympathetic appraisal of Boiardo came, some time later, the more favorable opinion of the poet-scholar Carducci, who considered Boiardo "uno de' piú grandi poeti italiani". [10] While De Sanctis felt that Boiardo "concepì il suo poema da pedante e per obbedire a pedanti," [11] Carducci, instead, believed that Boiardo "credeva a' suoi cavalieri e gli amava." [12]

Among the positivist critics of the late nineteenth and early twentieth centuries, the most admiring was Pio Rajna, who considered Boiardo second only to Dante. Rajna felt that Boiardo's language needed only a "spolverata" [13] and that in the perfidious Italy of Lodovico il Moro and Alexander VI the *Innamorato* was charged with "un alto valore morale." [14] In addition Rajna is credited with having "chiaramente impostato il problema della cavalleria, considerata finalmente in relazione alle personali tendenze del poeta, non come istituzione storica." [15]

In the present century Boiardo's lyric poetry and minor works, as well as the *Innamorato*, have been the object of renewed interest. In addition to those critical views mentioned in the course of this study there is the view of Benedetto Croce (and the objections to it) that Boiardo was essentially inspired by a love for the "energico" and the "primitivo." [16] This view has been shared

---

[8] Francesco De Sanctis, *La poesia cavalleresca e scritti vari*, ed. Mario Petrini (Bari, 1954), p. 74. Cf. *Storia*, p. 369.
[9] *Ibid.*, p. 75.
[10] Ponte, p. 281.
[11] *La poesia cavalleresca*, p. 62.
[12] Ponte, p. 281.
[13] Pio Rajna, "L'Orlando innamorato di Matteo Maria Boiardo," in *Studi su Matteo Maria Boiardo* by various authors (Bologna, 1894), p. 145.
[14] *Loc. cit.*
[15] Ponte, p. 282.
[16] Benedetto Croce, *Ariosto, Shakespeare e Corneille* (Bari, 1920), p. 68.

to some extent by Edmondo Rho and Emilio Bigi, and rejected by Virgilio Procacci. Giulio Reichenbach and Luigi Russo consider Boiardo a poet of adventure, who is inspired not only by the "energico" and "primitivo" but by love and the pleasure of narration itself. Angelandrea Zottoli has seen the poet's narrative as closely tied to the tastes of the Este Court and has stressed the idea that the *Innamorato* was written for the court as a *trattenimento*. Emilio Bigi also emphasizes this practical function of Boiardo's Poem.

Of the more recent studies which are wholly or partially concerned with the *Orlando innamorato* the more interesting are a philological study by Pier Vincenzo Mengaldo (cited below), a study of sources by Rosanna Alhaique Pettinelli,[17] and the stimulating analysis of Robert Durling, to which repeated reference is made below.[18]

---

[17] Rosanna Alhaique Pettinelli, "L'Orlando Innamorato e la tradizione cavalleresca in ottave; I. Raffronti di personaggi e situazioni," in *Rassegna della Letteratura Italiana*, Series 7, 71 (1967), pp. 383-418.

[18] The latest surge of interest in Boiardo has produced the substantial collection of essays *Il Boiardo e la critica contemporanea. Atti del convegno di studi su Matteo Maria Boiardo*, ed. Giuseppe Anceschi (Florence: Olschski, 1970), and various other studies, including, most recently, a thought-provoking article by Eduardo Saccone ("Osservazioni su alcuni luoghi dell'*Innamorato*," *MLN*, 86 (1971), 31-60), in which the author rejects the view of the *Innamorato* as an idyllic idealization in order to emphasize "la tensione, il *gioco* tra due realtà *nel* poema... (p. 59)." Saccone suggests that the Poem can be considered "... un'esemplare testimonianza di una crisi storica che proprio il 1494, l'anno della discesa di Carlo VIII e della morte di Boiardo, vide apertamente scatenarsi (p. 60)." See also in the same issue of *MLN* (pp. 114-122) Saccone's review of the *Atti* cited above.

Chapter One

THE POET AND HIS AUDIENCE

> Galeotto fu il libro e chi lo scrisse.
> (*Inferno* V, 137)

1. *Parataxis and Poeticopraxis*

When Giovanni Boccaccio takes up his quill to write the *Decameron*[1] his unannounced intention is to break the didactic chain of *terza rima* which links his world to Dante's. His declared intent is much more modest. In the *Proemio* he says he only wishes to succor, in as pleasant and instructive a way as he can offer, the idle lovelorn ladies imprisoned in their rooms with too much time to contemplate their sad states. These idle ladies, though they can surely afford the luxury of idleness, neither enjoy their leisure nor even succeed in satisfactorily occupying their idle time in such a way as to dispel the melancholic thoughts (induced by the "focoso disio" of love) which may trouble them in those quiet hours, since they are "quasi oziose sedendo" not by their own decision but because of the wishes of one or another member of their families. Not all of these ladies, however, need distraction such as the author can offer, for they are well satisfied by more readily accessible forms of diversion such as "l'ago, il fuso e l'arco" (needle, spindle and reel). The author's stories are written not for them but "in soccorso e rifugio di quelle che amano," and he tries to

---

[1] All citations of Boccaccio are to *Il Decameron*, ed. Charles S. Singleton, 2 vols. (Bari, 1955).

make the readings as purely enjoyable as possible, not even daring to burden the *dilicate* readers with classifications of genres. They may read with no *serious* thought given to the formal nature of what they read for the author cares little whether his stories are called "novelle, o favole o parabole o istorie" or whatever else the reader may wish to label them. Furthermore, in conclusion, to emphasize that this work is written for idle ladies in love with no means of extinguishing the amorous flames which consume their thoughts, he says explicitly that it is not for *studianti*, who are primarily interested not in passing time but in making good use of it. Thus one may not only label the stories as she sees fit, but, in addition, the author says in response to those critics who find some stories distasteful, the reader may select only those stories which promise to be more interesting judging by the summary of each graciously provided by the author himself.

This ostensible fracturability of the work is increased, and the separation from *terza rima* is further emphasized, by the inherently disconnected form of the narrative which results from the use of *idle* periodic sentences, each of which is an isolated conceptual unit in itself. Finally, this entertaining work, which was begun when the author was at last liberated from the bonds of love, as we learn in the *Proemio*, ends with a typical rhetorical "disclaimer of control"[2] over the contents of his work, saying that if he is criticized for his choice of vocabulary or stories he is only guilty of having conscientiously recorded what was related by the original storyteller — "ma io non potea né doveva scrivere se non le raccontate." The last word is, however, that if he were the inventor and writer of the tales, which he declares he is not, he would feel no shame if some should be considered less beautiful than others, since no craftsman, "da Dio in fuori," makes every product a model of perfection.

The presentation of the *Decameron* to idle ladies who need not worry about the structure and intellectual implications of the

---

[2] Robert M. Durling, *The Figure of the Poet in Renaissance Epic* (Cambridge, Mass., 1965). See especially Chapter V on Ariosto for a discussion of the use of this device by a Renaissance Poet. Since Durling's excellent chapter on Boiardo deals primarily with the relationship between Narrator and Audience, some of his observations will necessarily be repeated here. The technique of using capitals to distinguish between Narrator or Poet and author is adopted from this work, hereafter referred to as Durling.

work is, of course, purely polemical and defensive. Nevertheless it is necessary to preserve the notion of that original *fictional* readership in order to better appreciate how Boccaccio remains faithful to a medieval aesthetic which called for both *diletto* and *utilità* (but "was far from demanding unity of subject and inner coherence of structure in a work of literature"),[3] while at the same time allowing himself to mock the very medieval principles which his own work reflects. The distinction between a fictional and a real audience leads to a distinction between that work which is presented to idle ladies who need refuge, by one who claims *not* to be the author, and the work which is directed to the more reflective reader who is prepared to grasp its novel implications. One appeals to the heart, the other to the mind, but both are basically therapeutic. Hopefully, to be sure, the ideal reader gains both *diletto* and *utile consiglio* from a reading of a work which is most anti-didactic precisely when it is most delightfully instructive. Just as Dante's pilgrim is cured of a limp, all of Boccaccio's readers are cured of palpitations of the heart, be they caused by love or by other spiritual preoccupations.

Such apparent disregard for structural cohesion as is intentionally feigned in the posture of the author of the *Decameron* is often stressed as one of the unintended weaknesses of Matteo Boiardo's *Orlando innamorato*. Ignoring the undeniably paratactic nature of Boiardo's verse and considering only the looseness of structure in the poem as a whole, Robert Durling has suggested, however, that this lack of formal and ideological organicity may have been deliberate and significant, which would suggest that Boiardo intended to produce a non-significative anti-structure. Durling's conclusion is that "the fact that Boiardo should be accused of being an improvisor is ironic evidence of the success of the rhetorical self-representation of the Poet," whom he sees as representing "his own poetic activity as a kind of improvisation"[4] not unlike the spontaneous song of a young girl or a nightingale. Although the view of the Poem as an "improvisation" both intended and presented as such by the Poet is contestable (we shall

---

[3] Ernst Robert Curtius, *European Literature and the Latin Middle Ages*, trans. Willard R. Trask (New York, 1953), p. 501.
[4] Durling, pp. 104 & 107.

return to the question later), there is no doubt that the Poet wishes to elicit the same response of great pleasure from his audience as he experienced (II.19.1-3) upon hearing the sweet improvisations which delighted him, and he hopes that the season (Spring) will inspire him as it did the girl and the nightingale (II.8.1). It is no less clear that, because he is intent upon entertaining the audience with "new and delightful" song, he, like Boccaccio (who avoided categorizations), is careful not to tax the faculties of the audience with the "strenuousness of form" which is "foreign to the effect of spontaneity and the free indulgence in the moment that the courtly audience seeks."[5] Thus the Poet will not make "any comment on the formal significance of his transitions" when transporting the listeners from one interrupted episode to another. What he will do, to guard against anxiety, when he changes course abruptly, is to assure the audience that he will be able to find his way back at the appropriate time:[6]

> Tanto lunga tra lor fu la battaglia,
> Che altro tempo bisogna al ricontare.
> Adesso di saperla non ve incaglia,
> Ché a loco e a tempo ve saprò tornare;
> (II.3.16)

He does not require the same power of memory of the audience, however, that he himself exhibits, reassuring them that he will not be surprised if they have forgotten some past event, for he who wrote it barely remembers it (III.5.48). In addition, at the end of a long canto (I.12) the Narrator will say (jokingly, of course, as far as that completed canto is concerned) as Boccaccio did at the end of his work, that one need not read the whole: "Or questo canto è stato lungo molto; / Ma a cui dispiace la sua quantitate / Lasci una parte, e legga la mitate."

Leaving aside the question of the author's obligation before the principle of unity, it is safe to say that Boiardo's Narrator, like the Author of the *Decameron*, actively seeks to avoid any misunderstanding concerning the audience's obligation to him. He

---

[5] *Ibid.*, p. 108.
[6] All citations of Boiardo, except where otherwise indicated, are to *Orlando Innamorato, Amorum Libri*, ed. Aldo Scaglione, 2 vols. (Torino, 1966).

has no *avowed* didactic purpose, no *explicit* advice, and so he leaves the fictional audience with the clear understanding that their only obligation is to themselves, to be relieved, to be distracted from their distractions or simply to be entertained by spontaneous *diletto*.[7]

Just as Boccaccio compares his work to a *campo* which cannot by its very nature help but have in it some weeds mixed with "l'erbe migliori," so Boiardo's Poet says that his Poem is both like a bouquet of flowers from which the listener can pick his favorites, and like a garden planted with some thought to variety, since some will prefer one crop and others another:

> Còlti ho diversi fiori alla verdura,
> Azuri, gialli, candidi e vermigli;
> Fatto ho di vaghe erbette una mistura,
> Garofili e vïole e rose e zigli:
> Traggasi avanti chi de odore ha cura,
> E ciò che più gli piace, quel se pigli;
> A cui diletta il ziglio, a cui la rosa,
> Ed a cui questa, a cui quella altra cosa.
>
> Però diversamente il mio verziero
> De amore e de battaglia ho già piantato:
> Piace la guerra a l'animo più fiero,
> Lo amore al cor gentile e delicato.
>   (III.5.1-2)

In the end, as we see here, the Poet's garden really only offers two "plants", *amore* and *battaglia*, the roses of love for the more delicate, the thistles of war for the bold.

If Boccaccio's stories are from the beginning offered as a therapeutic for the ills which affect the idle love-sick, Boiardo's

---

[7] The importance of *diletto* has been commented upon by Durling (pp. 105ff.), and by Giulio Bertoni in *Nuovi studi su Matteo Maria Boiardo* (Bologna, 1904). Bertoni says (p. 168):

> Il Boiardo tratta la sua materia con una propria signorile disinvoltura proponendosi lo scopo di dilettare le dame e i cavallieri che debbono udirlo nella lussuosa Corte di Ferrara e sacrificando a questo scopo ogni altro fine.

Bertoni, as we see here, makes no distinction between Poet and author as Durling does, nor does he distinguish the frame audience from the Court of Ferrara. Durling does not make the latter distinction either.

poetry, which at first is only an offering of "cose dilettose e nove," later becomes the same sort of remedy, not only for the audience but also for the Poet, who offers the listeners a cure for "ogni affanno ed ogni pensier grave" (II.31.1) as he assures them that he himself has been relieved of "ogni noia ed ogni mal pensiero" (II.31.2) through his entertaining them. Thus we have two parallel situations — an Author linked through Love to his audience, desirous of attending to their needs and pleasure, careful not to make demands on them and apparently nonchalant about the totality of the creation of which he (Boiardo here is in line with Boccaccio, Cervantes and Manzoni, at least) is and yet is *not* the creator since the whole is presented as a translation or transcription of another source, in Boiardo's case the *True Chronicle* of Turpin.

2. *Word Heard and Written*

In addition to presenting his audience with a fragmented, loosely structured work, Boiardo further confuses the presentation by remaining ambiguous about the morphological nature of the poem. The best critics conclude that it is a written work which is designed to give the illusion of oral delivery, but which fails through the negligence of the author, as reflected in explicit reference to a written poem. Reichenbach, for example, notes that "anche qualche esordio di canto conferma che si trattava di opera scritta, non recitata," [8] such as I.18.1:

> Nel canto qua di sopra avete udito
> Come Marfisa, quella dama acerba...

He underscores *qua di sopra* but apparently fails to notice the words immediately following — *avete udito* — or simply wishes to spare Boiardo the criticism of having produced an impossibility, namely a written poem which the audience hears recited. Likewise Durling asserts that "Sometimes Boiardo violates the illusion of recitation; the use of 'de sopra' in I.6.1 or I.7.1 implies that the audience is reading the poem." [9] What should be recognized is

---

[8] Giulio Reichenbach, *Matteo Maria Boiardo* (Bologna, 1929), p. 144.
[9] Durling, note 2, p. 248.

that there are not *occasional* references to a written work but many. To begin with, the whole *Orlando innamorato* is presented in the title as a translation "tradutto da la verace cronica de Turpino, Arcivescovo remense." The title's assertion, while often reconfirmed by the author, as when he states that Turpin wrote what he recites (I.13.16), or that he writes what Turpin says (II.24.7), is seemingly contradicted in the first canto of Book One when, in the opening octaves, the Narrator says that the audience will hear "cose dilettose e nove" as they desire because this is an account which Turpin kept hidden:

> Questa novella è nota a poca gente,
> Perché Turpino istesso la nascose.
> (I.1.3)

Immediately thereafter, however, in the following octave, the Poet begins with the story as taken from Turpin: "La vera istoria di Turpin ragiona...." Not even Boiardo could have such a short memory. This ambiguity prevails throughout as the Poet continually indicates that the account is both a written verse translation and a recitation. At times the Poet will say "di sopra," but more often "di sopra odisti" (I.6.1) or "come ho sopra detto" (I.7.1) and states explicitly that the story does indeed exist in book form (I.27.42; II.31.42; III.4.11; III.4.50, referring to the book he himself completed some days previously; and in I.3.69 we find "io scrivo" and the like.) There is, thus, no doubt that a text does exist and that Turpin is not the only one who writes. There is, however, no less doubt that the frame audience listens to the *canti*. The use of "de sopra" does not imply a reading audience, but a reading Narrator. What is quite clear is that the Narrator writes, reads and narrates. A reading narrator, or a *cantastorie* with a text, is not an impossibility, for as Vittorio Rossi points out "Non sempre egli [il cantastorie] diceva a memoria; talvolta leggeva...." [10] There are times when Boiardo's Narrator becomes so absorbed in the story that he forgets he is following a text:

> Ma già finito nel presente è il canto,
> Che non me ne ero accorto ragionando.
> (II.24.66)

---

[10] Vittorio Rossi, *op. cit.*, p. 412.

The Narrator begins relating his story by implying that he is the possessor of privileged information ("Questa novella è nota a poca gente," I.1.3) and by telling the audience not to be surprised by the content, a story of Orlando in love: "Non vi par già, signor, meraviglioso / Odir cantar de Orlando inamorato." At other times, however, he marvels at the claims made by Turpin's text as in I.1.74 where the cry of Angelica's four giants, evoked by Feraguto's refusal to respect the prearranged rules of competition in the duel with Angelica's brother, is so ferocious as to cause the earth to tremble for two miles around. Turpin says so, but to the Narrator it seems a *meraviglia*. Although he occasionally claims to write what Turpin had recorded (II.24.7, "Turpino il dice, ed io da lui lo scrivo,"), thereby justifying his action, at times he simply cannot accept the authority of the Archbishop of Reims, as on the question of the size of a wild elephant which Turpin claims was thirty hands high (II.28.31, "Lo autor il dice, ed io creder nol posso.") Thus, because a history must relate the truth (III.7.53, "Pur ne la istoria il ver se convien dire"), the Narrator is reluctant to offer information which is not supported by proof, despite the fact that Turpin is a reliable historian who, the Narrator most often feels, does tell the truth (II.7.1, "Ma Turpin, che dal ver non se disparte / Per fatto certo il scrisse alle sue carte.") The Narrator too wishes to be a judicious historian.[11] The call for proof, however, is usually intended to produce a comic effect. The situation is one in which proof is unattainable or, if attainable, superfluous. Concerning the size of elephant legs, for example, the Narrator is hesitant to accept Turpin's figure because he himself has never measured wild elephants' legs (II.28.36), and, of course, neither had Turpin done so. Elsewhere (III.1.35), when Mandricardo and a lovely *dama ioconda* enter nude a bed adorned with curtains, he will not speculate on what games were played inside, since there were no witnesses. He only repeats Turpin's undeniable assertion that the pavilion collapsed upon them. On another occasion (II.20.13), discussing the inordi-

---

[11] The pose of Boiardo's Poet is like that of the Narrator of the *Spagna*, who seeks to remain faithful to the historical account while, at the same time, adorning it "con mie dire" (XXI.1). See *La Spagna*, 3 vols., ed. Michele Catalano (Bologna, 1939-40).

nate use of make-up by some women, as noted by Turpin, he says that there is no way of verifying the statement and that all he knows about the practice is that it is current in his own day.

Perhaps because the Narrator is generally skeptical about the reliability of all ancient authors, as in II.28.13, where he says "... non so se gli autor fosser ben giusti, / E scrivesseno il vero a' lor quaderni," he will sometimes tell the audience to believe whatever it likes (I.24.14) concerning even Turpin's version of history, and will protect himself as historical authority by placing the burden of credibility upon Turpin (II.27.12; II.29.12, "... se Turpin me dice il vero."). Dependence on the Archbishop's account, however, is constantly confirmed by reference to the book which the Narrator reads (II.30.38; II.1.5; II.13.58), and by reference to the Archbishop as the one responsible for the disposition of the material:

> Ma poi vi conterò questa aventura,
> E torno a Brandimarte e Fiordelisa,
> Come Turpin la istoria a me divisa.
> (II.19.15)

Frequently, as here, the Narrator must interrupt his tale because he is simply following Turpin (III.8.52; II.20.41; II.25.22; I.9.36). Once (III.2.54) he feels obliged to tell something because Turpin told it despite the fact that he feels it is unnecessary and that he would be embarrassed to tell it of his own accord.

With respect to himself as writer (presumably as author of the verse translation) the Poet makes frequent use of "inexpressibility topoi"[12] in telling the listeners what he writes (I.9.41); what he does not write (I.2.5); that some events are too strange for any written record (I.15.12); and that he is not sure of his ability to communicate in rhyme (II.20.48, "Ora io non vi saprei contare in rima..."), doubting that anyone could do so in certain cases. Sometimes there is no doubt he cannot express himself adequately, as when appears a dragon so terrible he cannot say how much so:

> Ecco fuor di quel monte esce un dragone,
> Terribil tanto, ch'io nol posso dire.
> (I.24.43)

---

[12] Curtius, *op. cit.*, pp. 159-162.

There are instances when he acknowledges his inability to describe the beauty of some woman in verse (II.15.52), or he cannot tell his story without assistance from a Muse (II.30.42), or he needs an iron tongue to describe a particularly violent battle (II.24.10), or he doubts that anyone could do the job (II.31.19), or he knows no one can adequately re-create the scene (II.10.26-27).

Although it is true that the Poet often moves from one episode to another without making "any comment on the formal significance of his transition," as already suggested, this is not an indication that the Poem is offered as a "spontaneous outpouring" or that the Poet is asserting "his whims in the arrangement of the poem."[13] On the contrary, when he does comment on his transitions, the Poet, aware of the episodic nature of his material, will express a *need* to return to the main theme, as in II.17.38:

> Or lasciamo costor tutti da parte,
> Ché nel presente ne è detto a bastanza,
> Però che il conte Orlando e Brandimarte
> Mi fa bisogno di condurli in Franza,
> Accioché queste istorie che son sparte,
> Siano raccolte insieme a una sustanza;
> Poi seguiremo un fatto tanto degno
> Quanto abbia libro alcuno in suo contegno.

The implication is that of a hierarchical relationship between the principal theme and the very numerous episodes which surround it. Once the main account is re-established the Poet will unhesitatingly indulge the audience in a new episode. The statement is thus an expression of a need for unity and control, and even implies that the many episodes surrounding the main line are not improvisations at all, but accounts which the Narrator already has in mind, as here he thinks of one which is of incomparable excellence. The lack of comment at transition may indeed be an indication that the shift is not dependent so much upon "whim" as upon fidelity to the original record which the narrator supposedly presents, namely, *La Verace Cronica De Turpino* of the title. The contradiction between the title's declaration that this is Turpin's own account and the statement in I.1.3 that Turpin kept

---

[13] Durling, pp. 96 & 98.

the story hidden is easily resolved if we distinguish between Turpin's *official* Chronical which does not mention Orlando's love and a *true* account, the integral "verace cronica" which does contain the *innamoramento* of Orlando, and which is the basis of the Poet's verse translation. The Poet is not the creator of an imaginary improvisation at all, but one who conscientiously strives to preserve his fidelity to the truth, an historical truth.

The Poet does compare himself to a young girl singing (II.19.1-3), but only to suggest again his own modest view of his ability to express himself adequately, in a pleasing manner. A true implication of the passage, seen against the background of the entire Poem, would be that the Poet-Translator's task is infinitely more difficult than that of the singing girl who gives no thought to content. The evidence which Durling finds in the following passage to support his view that the poem is presented as "just a spontaneous outpouring" is not at all conclusive:

> Tra bianche rose e tra vermiglie, e fiori
> Diversamente in terra coloriti,
> Tra fresche erbette e tra soavi odori
> De gli arboscelli a verde rivestiti,
> Cantando componea gli antichi onori
> De' cavallier sì prodi e tanto arditi,
> Che ogni tremenda cosa in tutto il mondo
> Fu da lor vinta a forza e posta al fondo;
>
> Quando mi venne a mente che il diletto
> Che l'om se prende solo, è mal compiuto.
> Però, baroni e dame, a tal conspetto
> Per dilettarvi alquanto io son venuto;
> E con gran zoia ad ascoltar vi aspetto
> L'aspra battaglia de Grifone arguto
> E de Aquilante....
>
> (III.3.1-2)

"Cantando componea," which is the sole expression of the Poet's function, more convincingly suggests that in his singing (translating into verse) the Poet is concerned not with inventing spontaneously (*inventio*) but rather with attending to the proper disposition and presentation of the material (*compositio*), as would be proper in a work which, if it is dependent upon the *ingenium* of the Poet for its style, is most dependent upon the *iudicium* of

Turpin for its content. Thus, unlike the *donzella*, the Narrator can deliver the truth in a controlled yet pleasing manner.

Certainly the content is not all Turpin's, for the Poet-Translator adds his own gloss to the text either in a quick comment or, more effectively, in a form which is not exceptional in epic and which was "regarded as a special elegance" [14] in the Middle Ages, that form being the digression (*egressio, excessus*). Such a digression appears when in the course of listing the infidel kings of Spain who oppose Charlemagne the Poet says that none will come from Biscaglia (Viscaya) since that region is ruled by the good Christian King Alfonso of Aragona "Di cui la stirpe e 'l bel seme iocondo / Non Spagna sol, ma illuminato ha il mondo" (II.23.6). The encomiastic digression is not concealed but acknowledged as such by the Poet as he explains that truth and affection have led him off course (II.23.8): "Or veritate ed anco affezïone, / Me ha tratto alquanto de la strata mia." It would thus seem that the Poet is giving his medieval subject an appropriately medieval treatment, for, as Curtius points out, "the medieval conception of art does not attempt to conceal digressions by transition — on the contrary, poets often point them out with a certain satisfaction." [15] When he returns to his register of persons and their provenance the Poet employs his own sense of judgment in eliminating as unessential the long list of names of those who will only be named again in a short while in the course of the battle. Except for these minor modifications the Narrator appears not to deviate from the authority of the true Chronicle of Turpin, and he certainly never claims to invent the story himself. [16] If he has difficulties in expressing himself, his difficulties lie in determining not *what* to say but *how* to say it in verse — "Ora io non vi saprei contare in rima."

The Poem thus presents a situation in which the Narrator surely reads from a text, but with indications that his task involves

---

[14] Curtius, pp. 501-2.

[15] *Ibid.*, p. 502.

[16] Occasionally the Narrator uses the verb *divisare* to describe his function (II.1.15, "... in questo libro io ve diviso"; III.7.6, "Or odeti la istoria che io diviso"), but it is clear that he does not intend it to mean "devise" or "invent". This is evidenced by the fact that the same verb describes Turpin's activity (II.19.15, "Come Turpin la istoria a me divisa) indicating that it refers to the presentation of the material, not its invention.

certain difficulties of expression, and that, as any Poet might, he wishes to be eloquent and entertaining. As for the audience there is no doubt that they listen, for if the Poet says "di sopra odisti" or "aveti odito" (I.1.42) or "sentisti" (I.11.47), he never says "di sopra avete letto." The frame audience never reads, although the Poet does not exclude the possibility that other audiences will read.[17] The entire structure of the Poem is a balance between written word and spoken word. The form is essentially popular and oral, but Boiardo fused it with a written tradition, just as many of his episodes he made "a welding together of the two elements, the Classical and the popular."[18]

Undoubtedly Boiardo did conceive of the *Orlando innamorato* as a written work intended for publication. Printing was initiated in Ferrara in 1471, as Bertoni tells us,[19] and flourished under Ercole I, and it was the author himself who supervised the 1483 edition of Books One and Two.[20] In addition the Poem had already circulated in manuscript form.[21] Nevertheless, it is also certain that Boiardo conceived of the Poem as an oral experience, since as Zottoli points out:

> A leggere il poema, si vede che, per ridar la misura a più d'un verso zoppicante, come per pareggiare le altre scabrosità che la scrittura trasandata presentava allo sguardo, Boiardo doveva fare un grande assegnamento sulla recitazione, anzi, se si ha presente qualche rima che con una corretta pronuncia italiana non tornerebbe in nessun

---

[17] At the end of Canto 12, Book One he does use the verb *leggere*, but since the frame audience has already heard the canto, it obviously refers to some other audience.

[18] Colbert Searles, "The Leodilla Episode in Bojardo's Orlando Innamorato," *Modern Language Notes*, 17, No. 7 (November, 1902), p. 205, column 410.

[19] Giulio Bertoni, *La biblioteca estense e la coltura ferrarese ai tempi del Duca Ercole I* (1471-1505), (Torino, 1903), p. 36.

[20] Although this edition of his own poem was printed in Reggio, Boiardo was so interested in printing as to want to establish a printing operation in Scandiano, where he spent most of his leisure writing time. Such an interest is not surprising considering that movable type was invented only some thirty years earlier.

[21] Reichenbach (*op. cit.*, p. 141) points out that Andrea da le Vieze on March 1, 1479 had already begun copying the poem, as confirmed in a letter written by Andrea to Ercole I.

modo, sopra una recitazione passante attraverso una glottide emiliana.[22]

In analysing the Poet's relationship with his audience we see that there may be a conscious intent in the juxtaposition of oral and written elements. The tension which is produced by that juxtaposition is the dialectical element which links the crystallized historicity of the chivalric world with the harmonious totality of the transcendent romanesque dream. The historical past becomes the Symbolic mirror which links the Real with the harmonious vision of the Imaginary as the audience becomes its ideal self.

3. *The Audience*

It has been rightly pointed out that "the most interesting and original aspect of Boiardo's use of the figure of the poet" lies in his representation of the relation between the Poet and his audience."[23] Yet the preconceived notions of the best critics, the one quoted included, may have prevented us from seeing precisely what the relationship is.

The audience for which our Poet narrates his romance is an idle audience, descendants of the idle ladies of Boccaccio's readership and ancestors of Cervantes' *desocupado lector*. Unlike Boccaccio's ladies, who were not *oziose* by choice, and unlike Matteo Boiardo, who was condemned to a sedentary role by gout, the Poet's audience in the *Orlando innamorato* meets willingly to hear "cose dilettose e nove." They are *oziosi*, as are the Christians and Saracens who gather at Charlemagne's court in peaceful coexistence, and their *ozio* implies a certain freedom from concern, as does that "ocio amoroso" (Sonnet 44) of Boiardo's *Canzoniere* which leaves the soul "rimota da ogni pensier vile." In the Poem Love comes in such an idle moment to the great warriors of Orlando's world gathered at Charlemagne's banquet; it even comes to the King himself. Most accept that Love eagerly, but Orlando, in accepting, thinks himself mad for doing so. The fact remains,

---

[22] In his Introduction to *Tutte le opere di Matteo M. Boiardo*, ed. Angelandrea Zottoli, 2 vols., 2nd. ed. (Milan, 1944), p. XX.
[23] Durling, p. 98.

however, that he and all others present believe they have been struck by the rays of love and, according to the Narrator, Orlando has been wounded more deeply than all others. It will be interesting to see what effect the story of Orlando's enamorment has on the listeners who have willingly fallen into a state of idleness.

The audience comes to hear the Poet in the day, probably in the afternoon (II.28.1, "Segnori e dame, Dio vi dia bon giorno"), they come only to listen (II.11.1, "Seti adunati sol per ascoltare) and they leave before nightfall (II.8.12, "E, per non vi tenir a notte scura..."). The listeners ask questions (II.29.12), their pleasure is reflected in their faces (II.27.2; III.9.1) and they enjoy listening, as the Poet frequently suggests, because of their nobility of being which matches that of the honored ancients:

> A voi piace de odir l'alta prodezza
> De' cavalieri antiqui et onorati,
> E 'l piacer vostro vien da gentilezza,
> Però che a quel valor ve assimigliati.
> Chi virtute non ha, quella non prezza;
> Ma voi, che qua de intorno me ascoltati,
> Seti de onore e de virtù la gloria,
> Però vi piace odir la bella istoria.
>   (II.13.2)

By the opening octaves of Book Three, Canto Nine, the court has been transformed into a new paradise in which dwell "queste genti angelice e divine." The expectation is not that these lovers will ascend into heaven (perhaps like Beatrice) but that the "Celestial Eros"[24] will descend incarnate and be seated at the center of this sensual domain as its eternal Majesty. If earlier Orlando has spoken of God as "la divina monarchia" (I.18.41) of the chivalric world, the Poet at this point is thinking in terms of a divine sensuality which rules the world of romance. In this world *diletto* is the main concern as the Narrator encourages all to put away disturbing thoughts, even when related to concern for Orlando's safety, and relax:

---

[24] Durling, p. 105: "Although the Poet speaks of love in terms of the Celestial Eros, it is clear that what he has in mind is no mystical *Askese*, but what he regards as a healthily sensual courtly love."

> Lasciati Orlando in quel tempo malvaggio,
> Né vi impacciati de sua mala sorte,
> Voi che ascoltando qua sedeti ad aggio:
> (II.8.63)

Although the Narrator occasionally wonders if he should not spend less time on certain topics (II.23.10), the prevailing impression is that the listeners have a lot of time to pass away, regardless of the subject.

Leading critics remind the reader that the *Orlando innamorato* was written for the court,[25] that the court for which it was written was the Este Court of Ferrara,[26] and that women figured prominently in that court,[27] with one of them (Isabella d'Este) having possibly exerted the greatest influence in encouraging the author to write his poem.[28] The critics then automatically assume that the frame audience represents the Court of Ferrara, complete with these prominent women. Panzini, for example, assumes the presence of women in the audience from the beginning: "'Signori e dame —comincia il Poeta—, Orlando era innamorato.'"[29] Likewise Bertoni says of the audience:

> E questi sono principesse, dame e donzelle delle più esperte nell'arte di farsi corteggiare e d'amare, letterati, dotti e poeti che sanno giostrare e caracollare destramente sul loro cavallo...[30]

More recently Robert Durling, in reference to the opening verses ("Signori e cavallier che ve adunati / Per odir cose dilettose e nove"), has said that "The Poet is thus represented as speaking to a group of gentlemen and ladies, who are often described as

---

[25] Angelandrea Zottoli, *Dal Boiardo all'Ariosto* (Milan, 1934), p. 57.
[26] See note 7 for Bertoni's statement.
[27] Bertoni, *La biblioteca estense*, p. 88.
[28] See Alessandro Luzio's "Isabella D'Este e L'Orlando Innamorato" in the collection of studies by various authors *Studi su Matteo Maria Boiardo* (Bologna, 1894). Although the *editio princeps* is dedicated to Ercole I, Luzio conjectures that Berni's dedication of the *Rifacimento* (his revision of the Poem) to Isabella indicates that "il Boiardo si proponeva realmente d'intitolare a lei la seconda e compiuta edizione del poema, che la morte interruppe." (p. 151).
[29] Alfredo Panzini, *Matteo Maria Boiardo* (Messina, 1918), p. 40.
[30] *La biblioteca estense*, p. 87.

sitting around him."[31] We are thus led to imagine a static situation from beginning to end with the same listeners possibly always seated in the same chairs. If the ladies are there in the beginning, however, they must be in the back row for the Poet certainly does not mention them. The composition of the audience is, contrary to what has been presumed, equivalent to that of the guests gathered around the table of Charlemagne. They are "Signori e cavallier" just as the notable guests of Charlemagne are all men. Indeed, whereas there is a passing reference to Orlando's wife Alda and other women being present somewhere in the banquet hall (I.1.22), no such reference is made to women being present in the Poet's audience. The fact that they attain prominence only much later suggests that between the "Signori e cavallier," the idle men, of Boiardo's first verse, and the knights of Ariosto's opening verse (who are not listeners, but armed heroes of the action surrounded by women — "Le donne, i cavallieri, l'arme, gli amori") there is a movement from the cavalleresque world of men toward a world of "genti angelice e divine" (equal in divine beauty to Angelica) who wait to receive the God of Love just as Charlemagne's court received Angelica. At one point the action of the story arouses sentiments in the listeners equal in dignity and worth to the performance of the heroes, so as to indicate that they are, if not actually involved in the action, at least in sympathetic harmony with those heroes:

> Così ad ogni atto degno e signorile,
> Qual se raconti, di cavalleria,
> Sempre se allegra lo animo gentile,
> Come nel fatto fusse tuttavia,
> Manifestando fuor il cor virile
> Quel che gli piace e quel ch'egli disia;
> Onde io di voi comprendo il spirito audace,
> Poi che de odirme vi diletta e piace.
> (II.24.2)

Just as Orlando is perpetually deprived of reaching his goal in his quest for Angelica, so too the listeners, equally pertinacious, readily follow the Narrator as he apparently moves with equally

---

[31] *Op. cit.*, p. 92.

fortuitous motivation from one unfinished episode to another. Far from being an obstacle to mere vicarious satisfaction, however, the Poet will appear in the role of mediator between his audience and the pleasures of a more immanent world of amorous desire. [32]

In the opening scene, as we have said, the listeners appear as gentlemen and cavaliers who are told not to be surprised to hear tell of Orlando in love. In the early stages of the narration these listeners are addressed only as *segnor*. The Poet helps them to associate more easily with the deeds and heroes of the past by such devices as calling Ranaldo "il baron nostro" (I.4.85) or by use of the historical present tense of the verb (I.4.89). In the early cantos of the Poem the listeners are exposed to thoughts of adventure, battle, love and incantation. In Cantos 18 and 19 of Book One, suddenly, when the Poem reaches its epic high-point in a battle inspired by love, the revelation of the supremacy of Love over Arms and the manly art of warfare is accompanied by a transformation in the audience.

In Canto 18 begins the justly famous duel between Orlando and Agricane, King of Tartaria, a duel which belongs to the category of amorous conflicts mentioned in the opening octave of Canto 19. The two warriors display the highest regard for chivalric sentiment until Love distorts their perspective. Agricane pretends to flee from the battlefield (I.18.31) so that he can confront Orlando, who follows him, alone in an isolated spot, thereby sparing him from suffering the shame of defeat when he asks Orlando to surrender. Agricane's noble intention in asking Orlando to surrender is to make it possible from him to spare Orlando's life. Orlando, on the other hand, wonders why Agricane would flee and thus, by trying to prolong his life a while, as he suspects, acquire both death and shame at one stroke:

---

[32] Another indication of Boiardo's understanding of the operation of mediated desire is found in his treatment of characters who sometimes assume a narrative voice, as in the Leodilla episode (I.21-22). Leodilla, in relating the story of her jealous husband Folderico and her lover Ordauro, is aroused to the point (I.24.14-17) of half hoping Orlando will "assault" her. Cf. Giulio Reichenbach, *L'Orlando innamorato di M. M. Boiardo* (Firenze, 1936), p. 74: "... il racconto licenzioso ha acceso la fantasia della stessa narratrice...." Elsewhere Iroldo says (I.12.49) that jealous love is the highest form of passion in the world.

> —Come tanta vergogna pôi soffrire
> A dar le spalle ad un sol cavalliero?
> Forse credesti la morte fuggire:
> Or vedi che fallito hai il pensiero.
> Chi morir può onorato, die' morire;
> Ché spesse volte aviene e de legiero
> Che, per durare in questa vita trista,
> Morte e vergogna ad un tratto s'acquista.—
> (I.18.33)

When he learns the reason for Agricane's flight he too shows consideration by offering to baptize his opponent (I.18.36). But Agricane will not be baptized; he would rather fight Orlando than be king of Paradise. He is thoroughly a man of action; from childhood he has been an advocate of the active life:

> —E così spesi la mia fanciulezza
> In caccie, in giochi de arme e in cavalcare;
> Né mi par che convenga a gentilezza
> Star tutto il giorno ne' libri a pensare;
> Ma la forza del corpo e la destrezza
> Conviense al cavalliero esercitare.
> Dottrina al prete ed al dottor sta bene:
> Io tanto saccio quanto mi conviene.—
> (I.18.43)

He has only contempt for books (especially poems, one would imagine) and is not convinced by the argument in favor of study presented by Orlando, who also agrees that "l'arme son de l'omo il primo onore."

After Orlando and Agricane have declared a temporary truce because of darkness, intending to resume the duel in the morning, they lie down to sleep in the woods near a fountain, confident of each other's respect for the truce. The fierce warriors now calmly converse in the darkness, with Agricane, however, being willing only to talk of arms or love. As the conversation turns to the topic of love the two men learn that they are both enamored of the same woman, Angelica. Agricane insists that Orlando give her up, for he cannot tolerate the thought that another man even thinks of her; but, of course, Orlando refuses. Thus, despite the darkness, the duel resumes, but the confrontation is immediately interrupted for the audience as the canto ends on the verge of the most ferocious love-inspired duel in history, with Orlando no longer confident that the great King Agricane will adhere to the accepted code of chivalric conduct (I.18.54).

The next canto begins in a manner very much like the Poem's opening octave, except that now the gentlemen in the audience are "inamorati" and the presence of women is confirmed for the very first time:

> Segnori e cavallieri inamorati,
> Cortese damiselle e grazïose,
> Venitene davanti ed ascoltati
> L'alte venture e le guerre amorose
> Che fer' li antiqui cavallier pregiati,
> E fôrno al mondo degne e glorïose;
> Ma sopra tutti Orlando ed Agricane
> Fier' opre, per amore, alte e soprane.
> (I.19.1)

The canto thus opens, as if by incantation, with the instantaneous metamorphosis of the gentlemen listeners into lovers accompanied by ladies. The same canto ends appropriately with Brandimarte throwing away his helmet and shield (I.19.57) and going off with his lady, Fiordelisa, into the only sensual and spontaneous love scene of the Poem as Brandimarte "con essa in braccio si colcò su il prato (60)." The last octave of Canto 19 presents a *voyeur* (another audience) who shortly will abduct the girl. He is a thoroughly concupiscent old hermit whose own sexual desires are aroused by watching the lovers (*visio corporalis est principium amoris sensibilis*.) In addition, the amorous achievement of Brandimarte is further accentuated by the shame he felt before encountering Fiordelisa when his friends came to assist him in his battle with a woman, Marfisa, whom neither he nor they could defeat. The Narrator comments ironically that his face was red with shame (I.19.56) out of embarrassment not for himself, who is stopped by nothing, but for his rescuers who collectively cannot defeat Marfisa.

From Canto 20 on the Narrator addresses his audience only as *Segnori* or *bei Segnori* (I.23.1; I.26.64; I.27.62) or *Cari segnori* (I.28.54) or *Bella brigata* (II.3.70) until Canto Eight of Book Two, which begins in a traditional Provençal manner with the language of courtly love:

> Quando la terra più verde è fiorita,
> E più sereno il cielo e grazïoso,
> Alor cantando il rosignol se aita
> La notte e il giorno a l'arboscello ombroso;
> Così lieta stagione ora me invita
> A seguitare il canto dilettoso,
> E racontare il pregio e 'l gran'onore
> Che donan l'arme gionte con amore.
>
> Dame legiadre e cavallier pregiati,
> Che onorati la corte e gentilezza,
> Tiratevi davanti ed ascoltati
> Delli antiqui baron l'alta prodezza,
> Che seran sempre in terra nominati:
> Tristano e Isotta dalla bionda trezza,
> Genevra e Lancilotto del re Bando;
> Ma sopra tutti il franco conte Orlando,
>
> Qual per amor de Angelica la bella
> Fece prodezze e meraviglie tante,
> Che 'l mondo sol di lui canta e favella.

The ladies of the audience are again mentioned; they have, in fact, replaced the "cavallieri" in first position. They are linked by suggestion to Tristan and Iseult, Guinivere and Lancilot and Orlando and Angelica, among the most exemplary models of passionate lovers ever recorded. Thus, as the Poem's characters, inspired by Angelica's beauty, move from the virginal cavalleresque historicity of the carolingian world (all the Christian paladins are of the carolingian cycle) into a spontaneous romanesque fantasy in which they swear fealty to the Lord of Love, the Poet is able to seduce the listeners from their detached reality and submerge them in an idealized world of amorous attachment, just as Orlando in the very same Canto (II.8) is forcibly thrown into the lake of the fata Morgana, or as later (II.31) he descends into the River of laughter into a world of perpetual dream-like joy. If a moment of care-free idleness leads to Charlemagne's guests becoming the prisoners of Love, such an idle moment proves to be no less a danger to the Poet's audience as the past becomes a source of emulation as well as admiration for the present.

From this point to the end of the Poem the presence of the ladies in the audience is not neglected; the listeners are *Segnori e dame* (II.28.1) until the last octave of the Second Book, where with a flourish the Poet completely transfigures them into lovers as the "Segnori" and "cavallieri" disappear from the scene:

> A voi, legiadri amanti e damigelle,
> Che dentro ai cor gentili aveti amore,
> Son scritte queste istorie tanto belle
> Di cortesia fiorite e di valore;
> Ciò non ascoltan queste anime felle,
> Che fan guerra per sdegno e per furore.
> Adio, amanti e dame pellegrine:
> A vostro onor di questo libro è il fine.
> (II.31.50)

Through a book the purpose of which is to honor gentle lovers, the idle cavaliers have been elevated beyond the harsh reality of the *anime felle*, and if, near the end, the tempestuous battles become somewhat monotonous, as some critics feel, a perpetual infernal tempest devoid of spontaneity, this is merely part of the contrast between the world of love, in which arms are used to serve the desired object, and the world of ire, where they are used to vanquish what is desired. (One might speculate that in the real world the pen was for Boiardo no less heavy than the sword when employed to write the many officious letters required of him.) In contrast to those who know nothing about the ideals of Love, Honor and Glory, those who fight only "per sdegno e per furore," the audience appears even more worthy to hear tell of courtesy and valor, since they have attained the very gentility of being which is to be honored in this idealized account of Love and War. Their worlds are as opposed as are Orlando and Rodamonte, and at times it appears, as Durling says in reference to the following (p. 108), that "The romantic idealization of an impossible past withers in the wind (See III.1.1) of the exigencies of real life":

> Come più dolce a' naviganti pare,
> Poi che fortuna li ha battuti intorno,
> Veder l'onda tranquilla e queto il mare
> L'aria serena e il cel di stelle adorno;
> E come il peregrin nel caminare
> Se allegra al vago piano al novo giorno,
> Essendo fuori uscito alla sicura
> De l'aspro monte per la notte oscura;

> Così, dapoi che la infernal tempesta
> De la guerra spietata è dipartita,
> Poi che tornato è il mondo in zoia e in festa
> E questa corte più che mai fiorita,
> Farò con più diletto manifesta
> La bella istoria che ho gran tempo ordita:
> Venite ad ascoltare in cortesia,
> Segnori e dame e bella baronia.
>
> (III.1.1-2)

At this point, however, the "romantic idealization" has not yet withered, and, in fact, the Poet's optimism (II.31.49, "Non seran sempre e tempi sì diversi") is rewarded as the world turns "in zoia e in festa." Hence the battle is not yet decided as the "exigencies of real life" only serve to make the Poet's song even more delightful and the court, by contrast, appear "più che mai fiorita." By the time we have reached the Third Book we are so totally immersed in the romanesque dream as to assume that the present day courtiers are the heroes (the *saints*, nearly) of a royal paradise of Love. The Poem endures as long as the illusion exists of a world where "cortesia e valore" rule, where battles are initiated not through *sdegno* or *furore* but for idealistic reasons, where all actions are motivated only by *Amore* and *Gloria*. The illusion itself, and the faith of the Poet in that ideal world lasts, however, only as long as the Poet is reassured of the existence of a public which willingly desires to share the pleasure of that illusion. It is not surprising, therefore, that "It is with continual reference to this audience that the figure of the Poet is represented (Durling, p. 99)." The audience is absolutely essential to the perpetuation of the Poem for as the Poet himself confirms: (III.3.2) "...mi venne a mente che il diletto / Che l'om se prende solo, è mal compiuto."

Boiardo, it has been said, was not an escapist, but this subject lacks analysis. What appears as an opposition between present reality and the imaginary cavalleresque world of the past, it should be noted, is found only very late in the Poem (Cantos II.31 and III.9 especially). Earlier, in the opening octaves of Book II, the first comment on the value of the past indicates that the Poet's concept of the relationship between past and present is basically humanistic:

> Nel grazïoso tempo onde natura
> Fa più lucente la stella d'amore,
> Quando la terra copre di verdura,
> E li arboscelli adorna di bel fiore,
> Giovani e dame ed ogni creatura
> Fanno allegrezza con zoioso core;
> Ma poi che 'l verno viene e il tempo passa,
> Fugge il diletto e quel piacer si lassa.
>
> Così nel tempo che virtù fioria
> Ne li antiqui segnori e cavallieri,
> Con noi stava allegrezza e cortesia,
> E poi fuggirno per strani sentieri,
> Sì che un gran tempo smarirno la via,
> Né del più ritornar ferno pensieri;
> Ora é il mal vento e quel verno compito,
> E torna il mondo di virtù fiorito.
>
> Ed io cantando torno alla memoria
> Delle prodezze de' tempi passati.
> (II.1.1-3)

In the Spring of human virtue, in the days of the "antiqui segnori e cavallieri," the world was filled with "allegrezza e cortesia." As the seasons changed these virtues were for a time lost "per strani sentieri," only to await the advent of a new time "di virtù fiorito." This new age, the present, is not yet equal to the past and the Poet must return to the past for his models of perfection; but by so doing it is hoped that the past will become a model for the present to imitate, in an effort to restore the virtues of the past. The Poet's audience, we find, can honor the past by listening to the Poet's song (II.26.1-3). The benefit to ancient heroes is recalled by the humanistic concept of the virtue of the past surviving in the memory of the present, without which all its achievements would have been in vain. At this point the Poet cannot help but note the striking difference between the past, when Fame brought immortal life to contemporary heroes, and the present, which is so deficient in fame and virtue that the Poet's only choice is to continue immortalizing the giants of the past:

> Se a quei che trïonfarno il mondo in gloria,
> Come Alessandro e Cesare romano,

> Che l'uno e l'altro corse con vittoria
> Dal mar di mezo a l'ultimo oceàno,
> Non avesse soccorso la memoria,
> Serìa fiorito il suo valore invano;
> Lo ardire e senno e le inclite virtute
> Serian tolte dal tempo e al fin venute.
>
>   Fama, seguace de gli imperatori,
> Ninfa, che a gesti e' dolci versi canti,
> Che dopo morte ancor gli uomini onori
> E fai coloro eterni che tu vanti,
> Ove sei giunta? A dir gli antichi amori
> Et a narrar battaglie de' giganti,
> Mercè del mondo che al tuo tempo è tale,
> Che più di fama o di virtù non cale.
>   (II.22.1-2)

Ultimately it is Fortune which determines the course of Fame as we are reminded when the Poet recalls the once great name of Carthage, which in modern times is scarcely remembered (II.27.45).

Following an invocation of Venus and Mars (II.12.1-2), the Poet observes that the present, in addition to lacking notable heroes, is also less "glorious" than it might be because arms have fallen into the hands of men far less worthy than the "omo gentile" of antiquity for whom Love and Battle were a privileged duty. Warfare, "quella arte degna ed onorata" (II.12.3), today has fallen "tra villani." The same sentiment is repeated in the closing octaves of Book Two:

> Mentre che io canto, non posa la mente,
> Ché gionto sono al fine, e non vi miro;
> A questo libro è già la lena tolta:
> Il terzo ascoltareti un'altra volta.
>
>   Alor con rime elette e miglior versi
> Farò battaglie e amor tutto di foco;
> Non seran sempre e tempi sì diversi
> Che mi tragan la mente di suo loco;
> Ma nel presente e canti miei son persi,
> E porvi ogni pensier mi giova poco:
> Sentendo Italia de lamenti piena,
> Non che or canti, ma sospiro apena.

> A voi, legiadri amanti e damigelle,
> Che dentro ai cor gentili aveti amore,
> Son scritte queste istorie tanto belle
> Di cortesia fiorite e di valore;
> Ciò non ascoltan queste anime felle,
> Che fan guerra per sdegno e per furore.
> Adio, amanti e dame pellegrine:
> A vostro onor di questo libro è il fine.
> (II.31.48-50)

The Poet is so distressed by the villainous reality of the *anime felle* that he is unable to continue as his mind restlessly wanders from his topic; with Italy full of laments he can barely sigh, let alone sing. There is, however, that feeling of optimism, noted earlier, a feeling that perhaps the present will become like the past, a feeling which, if temporarily it is sustained, seems nearly to have died by the time we have reached the final octave of the Poem.

The last eight lines of the *Orlando innamorato*, which notably have three rhyme words in common with the next to last octave of Book Two ("Alor con rime elette..." cited above), seem to echo by their solemn tone the prophecy of Savonarola, who, two years earlier in Florence, had warned a corrupt Italy of a divinely ordained invasion from beyond the mountains, saying: *Ecce gladius Domini super terram*:[33]

> Mentre che io canto, o Iddio redentore,
> Vedo la Italia tutta a fiama e a foco
> Per questi Galli, che con gran valore
> Vengon per disertar non so che loco;
> Però vi lascio in questo vano amore
> De Fiordespina ardente a poco a poco;
> Un'altra fiata, se mi fia concesso,
> Racontarovi il tutto per espresso.
> (III.9.26)

The *Galli* are not like the *anime felle* of Book Two, who historically, may represent the Venetian troops of the 1482-84 War between Venice and Ferrara, in which the Pope, Sixtus IV, was

---

[33] Cf. Roberto Ridolfi, *Vita di Girolamo Savonarola*, 2 vols. (Rome, 1952), I. 116 ff.

allied with Venice. If they are the Redeemer's army, as might be suggested by the apostrophe, come to deliver Italy from the bondage of sin, they come with just motivation, and understandably, with "gran valore." Under the leadership of Charles VIII, furthermore, they come as semi-allies of Ferrara through Lodovico Sforza of Milan (husband to Beatrice d'Este, daughter of Ercole), who called for Charles' entry into Italy.

Now, though he sees the invaders as valorous and possibly filled with righteous motivation, the Poet seems to have lost all hope of transfiguring his world; even if he has another chance to sing, his song will be brief. (Boiardo will, of course, not return to the dream world of the past, partly because of the overriding obligation to host the invading troops, as we learn from his letters of the period.) The flames and fire (*foco*) of the concluding verses of Book Two were still located (*loco*) in the author's mind, but in the final octave of the Poem, while the Poet does not know which precise *loco* is to be destroyed, he sees that the *fiama* and *foco*, with new laments, are spreading now over Italy. Hence, even though the *anime felle* have disappeared, the destruction is only more painfully real.

When reality just begins to become burdensome the Poet does once offer an escape from that reality:

>Il sol girando in su quel celo adorno
>Passa volando e nostra vita lassa,
>La qual non sembra pur durar un giorno
>A cui senza diletto la trapassa;
>Ond'io pur chieggio a voi che sete intorno,
>Che ciascun ponga ogni sua noia in cassa,
>Ed ogni affanno ed ogni pensier grave
>Dentro ve chiuda, e poi perda la chiave.
>
>Ed io, quivi a voi tuttavia cantando,
>Perso ho ogni noia ed ogni mal pensiero.
>   (II.31.1-2)

But the Poem is more than a simple escape mechanism, for we have seen that the Poet sings least precisely when the need to escape is greatest. Likewise it is more than an "opera pratica," a *dégradée* "letteratura di trattenimento... destinata a soddisfare i pratici gusti dei nobili gentiluomini della Corte estense" [34] for in the metamorphosis of the frame audience we see that the Poet is not interested in flattering those present by simply equating their virtue to that of the past, but rather in developing what latent potential they may possess. The world of the transfigured audience stands out against the harsh inescapable totality of life as a world which is gradually reduced to one amorous dimension, a world in which arms and noble deeds are subservient instruments of Love. Such a restriction of the world becomes an abstraction which dissolves under the pressure of a larger reality. The heavy intrusion of external reality destroys the dialectic between the Real (receptive) present and the Symbolic past; the *stade du mirroir*, the vision of harmony of Poet and audience, ends as their "pur monde enfantin" experiences the force of a menace which has become a true danger. [35]

The metamorphosis of the "segnori e cavallieri" into "leggiadri amanti e damigelle" is thus paralleled by a shift in viewpoint. If the early cantos of the Poem represent the delight of rediscovering the virtues of the past ("cose dilettose e nove"), the middle cantos advocate an imitation of those virtues, and the all too brief last book reflects the impossibility of relating that rarefied imitation to the totality of life, making of it not an idealistic pretext for examining life, but a transcendent abstraction devoid of relevance to reality, and possibly recognized as such by the author, who through the years found always less and less time to devote to his creation.

---

[34] Emilio Bigi, *La poesia del Boiardo* (Florence, 1941), p. 14.

[35] On Lacanian terminology see Jacques Lacan, *The Language of the Self; the Function of Language in Psychoanalysis*, translated with notes and commentary by Anthony Wilden (Baltimore, 1968). Wilden notes that for Lacan the Real (*le réel*) "is not synonymous with external reality, but rather with what is real for the subject." (p. 161). "Le pur monde enfantin" is Lukacs' definition of the epic; see Georges Lukacs, *La Théorie du Roman*, trans. Jean Clairevoye (Geneva, 1963), p. 54. On the dialectical relationship between alternate realities (or dream and reality) and the question of escapism, see the article by Eduardo Saccone, cited above, Introduction, note 18. See also Georg Weise, "Elementi tardogotici nella letteratura italiana del Quattrocento," *Rivista di Letterature Moderne e Comparate*, 10 (1957), 101-199, in which the author relates the "rapporti tra realtà e sogno poetico nell'*Innamorato* (p. 118)" to the phenomenon of Late-Gothic naturalism, and Aldo Scaglione, "Chivalric and Idyllic Poetry in the Italian Renaissance," *Italica*, 33 (1956), 252-260.

Chapter Two

INFLAMMATION OF THE HEART

Although Orlando is certainly the essential protagonist of the *Orlando innamorato*, in one sense we might say that the central figure of the Poem is no one individual, but an archetypal being which represents the entire community. That archetype is the Inflamed Soul, the *anima ardita* or *anima accesa*, which burns with a passionate fire sparked in the heart and fed either by *Ira* or *Amore*. The Poem is filled with examples of souls which are aflame with fires of varying purity, from those kindled by symbolic concupiscence (a desire for the sword, armor or horse of an illustrious knight) at one extreme, to those caused by lust at the other extreme. In the opening scene the purer flame of ire which drives the ablest of Christian and Saracen warriors to compete in a tournament for the simple prize of a wreath of roses (and the greater glory which it symbolizes) is contrasted with the flame which heats the covetous desire of King Gradasso, who will go to war to obtain the sword of Orlando and the horse of Ranaldo. Desire, under such conditions, becomes an obsession which allows for no substitution, not only for Orlando in his quest for Angelica, but even for Gradasso, whose desire is limited exclusively to possession of the sword Durindana and the horse Baiardo. King Gradasso does not desire Charlemagne's kingdom and wants the Christian King to remain his prisoner only for one day, until he can be exchanged for horse and sword:

> Io, che in Levante mi potea possare,
> Sono in Ponente per fama acquistare.

> Non certamente per acquistar Franza,
> Né Spagna, né Alamagna, né Ungaria:
> Lo effetto ne farà testimonianza.
> A me basta mia antiqua segnoria;
> Equale a me non voglio di possanza.
> Adunque ascolta la sentenzia mia:
> Un giorno integro tu con toi baroni
> Voglio che in campo me siati prigioni:
>
> Poi ne potrai a tua cità tornare,
> Ché io non voglio in tuo stato por la mano,
> Ma con tal patto: che me abbi a mandare
> Il destrier del segnor di Montealbano;
> Che de ragione io l'ebbi ad acquistare,
> Abenché me gabasse quel villano.
> E simil voglio, come torni Orlando,
> Che in Sericana mi mandi il suo brando.
>   (I.7.41-43)

Another case of obsession is that of Rodamonte, who exhibits the behavior of one who is inflamed by ire (excessive ire) to the point of living in perpetual rage, determined to eliminate, at all cost, peace on Earth. He characteristically accuses the less rash King Algoco, now quite old, of having lost his flame:

> Levossi in piede e disse: —In ciascun loco
> Ove fiamma s'accende, un tempo dura
> Piccola prima, e poi si fa gran foco;
> Ma come viene al fin, sempre se oscura,
> Mancando del suo lume a poco a poco.
> E così fa l'umana creatura,
> Che, poi che ha di sua età passato il verde,
> La vista, il senno e l'animo si perde.
>   (II.1.53)

Ire thus moves the individual to satisfy desires both noble and ignoble, in a quest for honor or glory through symbols and possessions, or in a drive for dominance, like that of Rodamonte, which resembles mad bestiality.

The flame of love too burns in souls whose desires reflect a vast range of inspiration, from the *concupiscentia oculorum* of the lustful old hermit who went off to pray and ended up, instead, abducting a lovely maiden (I.19) to the vision of spiritual beauty which marks the relationship between Ruggiero and Bradamante, whose love begins not with a *visio corporalis* but with Bradamante's interest in Ruggiero's heritage (III.5.17, "Chiedendo dolcemente e in cortesia / Che dir gli piaccia de che gente sia.") The physiological process of motivation involved in inducing the reaction of love is virtually identical to that which produces ire. For Boiardo's Poet ire is, as it was for Aristotle, characterized by an inflammation of the blood around the heart, an *accensio sanguinis circa cor*,[1] and love is, as it was for Ovid and later in the Provençal tradition, a burning *within* the heart. Traditionally, for Aristotle and for the Provençal poets, soul and body are inseparable elements in the process of emotional response; each emotion requires a particular kind of physiology, each kind of "form" must be embodied in a particular kind of matter.[2] It is for this reason that courtly love, for example, can only reside in a gentle heart. Boiardo adds to this tradition by suggesting that the effect of the inflammation depends only on the intensity of the flame, the particular combination of form and matter, but also on the mass involved, that is, on the size of the individual affected. He explains, humorously, that a short person, if he lacks size, has the advantage of having his members closer to the source of the flame, which makes him thus more *ardito*:

> De l'altro è Feraguto assai minore,
> Ma non gli lasciaria del campo un dito,
> Ché a lui non cede ponto di valore,
> Perché ogni piccoletto è sempre ardito;
> Ed èvi la ragion, però che il core
> Più presso a l'altre membra è meglio unito.
> (II.22.37)

The same Feraguto is also living evidence of the fact that the flames of ire and love can burn simultaneously in one breast (I.3.52, "Amore ed ira il petto gli infiammava.") An outward indication of the physical reaction to the inflammation produced by ire is seen in the affected person's face, which may become as red as fire (II.31.35).

Because the Poet's main topic is love, most of his statements on the physiological and psychological effects of cardiac inflam-

---
[1] *De Anima*, 403ª2 - ᵇ23.
[2] W. D. Ross, *Aristotle* (New York, 1963), pp. 130-131.

mation concern the type which is produced by *Amore*. This love can be characterized as an infectious disease which may attack anyone at anytime, young or old, rich or poor; it is a disease for which there is no remedy (I.28.2) and one which causes much suffering (I.17.52). Most often, however, it seems to be a malady of the proud; Orlando falls victim to it because of Pride:

> Ché qualunche nel mondo è più orgoglioso,
> È da Amor vinto, al tutto subiugato.
> (I.1.2)

Angelica is also a victim of Pride:

> Ché Amor vôl castigar questa superba.
> (I.3.40)

Thus the Poet suggests that, for Orlando and Angelica at least, *superbia* is the root of Love, just as in the Christian tradition it is the *initium omnis peccati* and the *radix omnium malorum*. If in the Christian system pride impedes the process of maturation of the individual through the infusion of love (*caritas*) here it serves to accelerate one's development, for *Amore*, like *caritas*, has the salubrious effect of "ripening" the individual. As Angelica says to Ranaldo (who by his aversion to her is being driven into a "loco oscuro e periglioso"), her life without his love would remain "sempre acerba e dura" (I.3.44-45). At the same time, in the case of Orlando, excessive *superbia* continues to lead to sin (alienation). Orlando's sin, however, is not against God but against Society, as we shall see.

One of the more serious effects of love as disease is its tendency to destroy the ability to reason (I.3.48) or to freeze the intellect at the same time that it burns the heart (I.27.45). It is perhaps because of this that Orlando feels led away from God by love (I.1.30) while at the same time he is led to a new paradise and a new beatific vision of Angelica asleep in the grass (I.3.70, "Sono ora quivi, o sono in paradiso?" he asks in bewilderment.) While the mind is weakened by love, the heart, we learn, is strengthened. Love gives "ingegno e sotigliezza" to the heart (I.22.29), as in the case of Leodilla and Ordauro, whose ingenuity (of the heart) enabled them to deceive Leodilla's old husband Folderigo in a typical provençal triangle involving a *mal mariée, fin aman* and *gilos*.

This love, which cannot be understood by one who has not felt it (I.12.10), is not clearly understood by the Poet himself, for his analysis abounds in contradictions, unless it is the nature of love to work in contrary ways. Although the Poet stated that all men can fall victim to love (II.9.47), we learn later that love never resides in an ignoble heart, "In petto villano amor non usa" (III.6.36), just as the soul of a fly, St. Thomas would say, never resides in the body of an elephant. Likewise, whereas love supposedly turns no good into evil, serving only to refine the already courteous heart (I.12.12) and making the lover always courteous (I.16.43, "Perché uno omo gentil e inamorato / Non puote a cortesia giamai fallire") it is love itself which causes Feraguto (I.1.83) and Ruggiero (III.6.34-35), the latter a master of courtesy, to disregard the rules of proper conduct. What seems best known about the nature of love is that its most virulent element is its tendency to fill the lover with the bitter torment of suspicion, an intense fear of all others as potential lovers of the same object of desire which sparks the flame of jealousy. Thus, as Iroldo tells Tisbina, jealous love is the most passionate form of love:

> Ma tu cognosci bene, anima mia,
> Che hai tanto senno e tal discrezïone,
> Che, come amor se gionge a zelosia,
> Non è nel mondo maggior passïone.
> (I.12.49)

The hottest flames of love are those in the heart of a loved-one who is rejected for another; accordingly we learn that the most venomous creature in the world is the jealous wife:

> Lo animal che è più crudo e spaventevole,
> Ed è più ardente che foco che sia,
> È la moglie che un tempo fu amorevole,
> Che, disprezata, cade in zelosia:
> Non è il leon ferito più spiacevole,
> Né la serpe calcata è tanto ria,
> Quanto è la moglie fiera in quella fiata
> Che per altrui sé vede abandonata.
> (I.8.37)

The *altrui* is an element which is often present, even if only in the imagination of the suspicious lover, as initially is the situation in the case of old Folderigo, who even fears the presence of male insects in the room of his wife Leodilla. It is the rival who accounts for the fact that it is more painful to give up something than to desire it without ever having it, as Iroldo so well knows after relinquishing his wife to the courteous Prasildo:

> Nel dolce tempo di mia età fiorita
> Fu' io di quella dama possessore,
> E fu la voglia mia sì seco unita,
> Che nel suo petto ascoso era il mio core.
> Ad altri la concessi alla finita:
> Pensa se a questo fare ebbi dolore!
> Lasciar tal cosa è dôl maggior assai
> Che desiarla e non averla mai.
> (I.17.3)

Even Orlando, when infected by jealousy, experiences the same reaction, for, as he says (I.25.53), "... perder l'acquistato è maggior doglia, / Che il non acquistar quel de che s'ha voglia." We know from Boiardo's *Canzoniere* (Sonnet 98) that a successful rival achieves divinity in the eyes of the jealous lover and becomes a "divo, a cui nullo altro e equale." With or without the rival present the nature of love is such that it leads the lover to hope always for better times (I.22.18) and is in no way diminished when left unrequited (I.9.41).

As far as Orlando is concerned, although his love and its consequences are the central theme of the Poem, the unanimous opinion is that he is not much of a ladies' man. The Poet portrays him as rather unattractive and the critics accuse him of every defect from unfamiliarity with acceptable courtship behavior patterns to simple physical insufficiency. His timidity as a lover, according to some critics, diminishes his stature as a hero in the eyes of the Poet. This misreading of the Poet's attitude toward his hero is due to the failure to see Orlando's love as problematic; that is, as an authentic personal sentiment desperately expressed through the lyric conventions of an amorous tradition which was not intended by its originators, the Provençal troubadours, to express such a sentiment. Orlando struggles to give his internal love-life an externalized form and has a difficult time doing it;

first because the conventional formulas are inadequate, and second because he is an inexperienced lover whose primary skill is that of being a *cavaliere*.

That Orlando is initially more a warrior than a lover is attested to by his appearance, which serves better to frighten giants than to attract lovely maidens. His voice is so fiercely proud that when he shouts it sounds inhuman (I.15.47). Although he is robust and strong, his wandering eye and thick eyebrows make him unattractive to some women, at least:

> E non doveti avere a meraviglia
> Se, più che 'l conte lei Grifone amava;
> Però che Orlando avea folte le ciglia,
> E d'un de gli occhi alquanto stralunava.
> Grifon la faccia avea bianca e vermiglia,
> Né pel di barba, o poco ne mostrava;
> Maggiore è bene Orlando e più robusto,
> Ma a quella dama non andava al gusto.
> (II.3.63)

Even asleep he is frightening to other knights, so "feroce e orribile" is his countenance (I.27.47). In addition, he is far from eloquent, since "per costume e per natura / Molte parole non sapeva usare," (II.20.59). He is more accustomed to fighting than to talking, and the wandering eye, the *occhio stralunato*, is itself an indication that he is most often inspired by *Ira* rather than *Amore*. The eye is a sort of professional deformation which serves as a permanent sign of his role. This is evident from the fact that when he becomes intensely overheated by Ire *both* his eyes wander, as when he battles the giant Zambardo:

> Per questo è il conte forte riscaldato
> Il viso gli comincia a lampeggiare;
> L'un e l'altro occhio aveva stralunato.
> Questo gigante ormai non può campare.
> (I.6.5)

Again later (II.24.56-57) he becomes "orribile a guardare" due to his "torcendo gli occhi de disdegno e de ira." The handsome Ranaldo shows the very same effect when he is inflamed by Ire:

> Dente con dente batte a gran furore.
> L'uno e l'altro occhio nella fronte ha torto.
> (I.4.58)

These are the typical symptoms of Ire, of Ire understood not only as the excessive reaction of "wrath" but of the state, beginning with the heating of the blood around the heart, which prepares the knight for battle, a condition which Ezra Pound, in another context, called "commotion." [3] That the warriors manifest precisely those symptoms indicative of Ire is confirmed by tradition. Saint Martin, for example, gives exactly these symptoms — boiling blood, chattering teeth, flashing flickering eyes (like Orlando's *viso lampeggiante* and *occhi stralunati*) and, in addition, trembling lips (P.L. 72.42-43, "flagrant et micant oculi, aestuat ab imis praecordiis sanguis, tremunt labia, comprimuntur dentes"). Thus, while the critics have thought that the Poet was intending to portray an ugly hero, the truth is that he was primarily intent upon giving him the appearance of a true warrior, a warrior who resembled not the gentleman courtier of the Renaissance but the medieval knight of the battlefield. That Boiardo's hero is outwardly modeled on a figure of the past rather than of the present is also reflected in his comportment as a lover.

Turpin calls Orlando a "mal scorto e sozzo amante" (II.3.66) when he attempts to converse with the deceptive Origille about love, and Zottoli finds in this appraisal a true disdain for Orlando on the part of the Poet, because he failed to give physical expression to his love for Origille. The critic says that Turpin called him "sozzo" because:

> Orlando, che non conosceva gli usi della buona società, amando in modo ingenuo, profondo, sincero, non osava certe intraprendenze dirette e disinvolte di cui le donne si lagnano ad alta voce, ma, a quanto si dice, o per lo meno a quanto Boiardo diceva, godono in segreto; egli era sozzo perché si perdeva in sospiri invece di andare al sodo. Noi siamo portati a chiamar sozzo chi certe intraprendenze si crede lecite, per Boiardo era sozzo chi se ne asteneva. [4]

Later Turpin will call Orlando a *babione*, a simpleton, for fearing to touch Angelica, and the Poet will add that he calls him so *de ragione* (II.19.50). It is surprising that Zottoli takes the judgments

---

[3] Ezra Pound, *Literary Essays* (New York, 1968), p. 174.
[4] Introduction to *Tutte le opere di M. M. B.* cited above, p. XXIV.

of the Archbishop, no avowed authority on the subject of courtship, as so seriously representative of the opinion of the Poet, for it is Zottoli himself who elsewhere [5] notes that it is precisely in connection with sex-centered situations that Turpin's "episcopale autorità" is invoked most effectively. The Poet's remark that Turpin calls Orlando a fool *de ragione*, with good cause, reflects as much upon the licentious Archbishop as it does upon the inexperienced lover. It is Turpin, not Boiardo, who in these instances prefers something more than unrewarding sighs.

More damaging to Orlando's reputation is the judgment of Siro Chimenz, who focuses primarily on the scene which brings Orlando and Angelica together in their most intimate encounter. Chimenz sees Orlando "per natura casto; non avverte, cioè, i richiami del senso erotico, anche se vicini e urgenti," and, therefore, he regards him as a victim of an "insufficienza fisica" whose sexual deficiency is compensated for by Orlando's "ardore ideale per la bellezza pura," in which the lady becomes a goddess to be adored. [6] Because of this viewpoint the critic sees Orlando's relationship with Origille, the figure of irresistibly seductive sensuality, an unpardonable inconsistency in the Poet's execution of Orlando's character. He does not see how an ideal sentiment for Angelica and a sensual desire for Origille can coexist in Orlando's heart. The fact that the Poet allows Orlando to be deceived by Origille more than once in nearly the same manner only underscores, for the critic, the failure of the Poet's representation. He is in agreement with De Sanctis to some extent that Orlando is not the hero but the "Pagliaccio" of the Poem. [7]

A re-evaluation of Orlando's relationship with Angelica and Origille, it seems clear, reveals that Orlando's behavior, if inconsistent, is not contrary to the formal attitudes and ideals of *his* age, and that what Chimenz sees as the behavior of one afflicted with an "anormalità sessuale" [8] may have been regarded, at another time, as abnormal only to the extent that it took a superior individual to adhere to a way of life which required such behavior.

---

[5] *Dal B. all'Ariosto* cited above, p. 66.
[6] Siro A. Chimenz, *La rappresentazione dell'amore nel poema del Bojardo* (Rome, 1931), p. 103.
[7] *Ibid.*, pp. 119-121.
[8] *Ibid.*, p. 112.

Orlando's love begins as an extension of the sentiment of the total community. His love originates in a totally organic world in which desire is only quantitatively variable.[9] When Angelica appears all are struck with love, Orlando more than the others:

> Ogni om per meraviglia l'ha mirata,
> Ma sopra tutti Orlando a lei s'accosta.
> (I.1.29)

> Ma a che dir più parole? Ogni barone
> Di lei si accese, ed anco il re Carlone.

> Stava ciascuno immoto e sbigotito
> Mirando quella con sommo diletto.
> (I.1.32-33)

In this closed totality exceptional behavior is attributable only to unnatural causes. Thus, the fountain of Hate which is the source of Ranaldo's aversion to Angelica is the product of incantation while the fount of Love which inspires Angelica to love Ranaldo is natural (I.3.33-38).

For an instant, at its inception Orlando's love for Angelica is the love of a married man; in fact, when he falls in love he does so in plain sight of his wife Alda. The Poet makes a point of comparing Angelica's beauty to that of Alda and the other ladies present. Alda does not object to her husband's behavior, which causes us to wonder if perhaps she does not find it perfectly acceptable. Traditionally there is only one known form of *Amore*, (excluding Christian Charity) which could be practiced by a married man toward a woman other than his wife without impropriety, and that was the *amor purus* of which Andreas Capellanus says:

---

[9] Cf. Lukacs, *op. cit.*, pp. 60-61: "En toute rigueur, le héros d'épopée n'est jamais un individu. De tout temps, on a considéré comme une caractéristique essentielle de l'épopée le fait que son objet n'est pas un destin personnel, mais celui d'une communauté. Avec raison, car le systèm de valeurs achevé et clos qui définit l'univers épique crée un tout trop organique pour qu'en lui un seul élément soit en mesure de s'isoler... la signification que peut revêtir un événement dans un monde clos de cette sorte reste toujours d'ordre quantitatif...."

> This love is distinguished by being of such virtue that from it arises all excellence of character, and no injury comes of it, and God sees very little offense in it. No maiden can ever be corrupted by such love, nor can a widow or a wife receive any harm or suffer any injury to her reputation.[10]

This is the *fin' amors*, the true love, of the provençal tradition which, as Maurice Valency says:

> ideally would involve a courtship of limited objective, resulting in a not quite adulterous relationship. Such love would not be, strictly speaking, sinful, illicit, or illegal. It pushed its frontiers to the very borders of adultery, but its merit was that it did not transgress them.[11]

If Orlando's love of Angelica, the Saracen Angel-lady, is externalized as this type of *fin' amors* which stops short of Venus' ultimate delight, he ought to be regarded not as an inferior lover with a severe physical handicap but as an immensely superior lover, a *fin' aman*. It only adds to the humor of the Poem if Orlando fulfills such a role primarily because he is simply inexperienced, and becomes an *amant malgré lui*. An analysis of Orlando's comportment reveals that he could easily qualify as a *fin' aman*, for the contrast between his courage on the battlefield and his timidity before women does not reflect an inconsistent personality but a more highly refined one. As Valency says:

> To be as stout as Launcelot in battle and as meek as Launcelot in love implied the possession of an exceptionally flexible personality, capable of assigning all the savagery of its aggressiveness to one sphere of activity, and all the charm of its passivity to another. It was a triumph of chivalric culture.[12]

Guillaume IX, Count of Poitier and Duke of Aquitaine, one of the earliest known troubadours, describes the knight of his *vers*

---

[10] Quoted from Maurice Valency, *In Praise of Love* (New York, 1958), p. 161.
[11] *Loc. cit.*
[12] Valency, pp. 163-4.

d'amor as being so timid as to be always fearful of angering or offending his lady:

> Ren per autruy non l'aus mandar,
> Tal paor ay qu'ades s'azir,
> Ni ieu mezeys, tan tem falhir,
> No l'aus m'amor fort assemblar;
> Mas elha'm deu mo mielhs tiar,
> Pus sap qu'ab lieys ai a guerir.[13]

Valency translates:

> I do not dare send word to her by another,
> so much I fear that it may make her angry
> nor do I myself dare to make a strong show
> of my love before her, so much do I fear
> to transgress; therefore she herself must
> find my remedy, since she knows that it is
> through her alone that I may recover.[14]

Orlando is from the beginning just such a timid knight. At the inception of love his heart trembles, he tries to conceal his desire and is embarrassed and shamefaced:

> Al fin delle parole ingenocchiata [Angelica]
> Davanti a Carlo attendia risposta.
> Ogni om per meraviglia l'ha mirata,
> Ma sopra tutti Orlando a lei s'accosta
> Col cor tremante e con vista cangiata,
> Benché la voluntà tenìa nascosta;
> E talor gli occhi alla terra bassava,
> Ché di se stesso assai si vergognava.
>   (I.1.29)

We are brought, in the final verse, to the formal conclusion of the courtly love tradition by an echo in that verse of a line by Petrarch, the last conscious *fin' aman*. In that tradition, as pure as pure love might be, it rarely accorded with the process of *caritas*, which subordinated love of woman to love of God. For this reason Orlando momentarily feels the weight of his error:

---

[13] R. T. Hill and T. G. Bergin, eds., *Anthology of Provençal Troubadours* (New Haven, 1957), *Mout jauzens*, stanza 8, pp. 7-9.

[14] Valency, p. 165.

INFLAMMATION OF THE HEART

> 'Ahi paccio Orlando!' nel suo cor dicia
> 'Come te lasci a voglia trasportare!
> Non vedi tu lo error che te desvia,
> E tanto contra a Dio te fa fallare?
> Dove mi mena la fortuna mia?
> Vedome preso e non mi posso aitare;
> Io, che stimavo tutto il mondo nulla,
> Senza arme vinto son da una fanciulla.
>
> Io non mi posso dal cor dipartire
> La dolce vista del viso sereno,
> Perch'io mi sento senza lei morire,
> E il spirto a poco a poco venir meno.
> Or non mi val la forza, né lo ardire
> Contra d'Amor, che m'ha già posto il freno;
> Né mi giova saper, né altrui consiglio,
> Ch'io vedo il meglio ed al peggior m'appiglio.'
>
> (I.1.30-31)

Thus unable to resist the power of love Orlando becomes the trembling cautious lover whom Turpin, who has a different concept of love, will call a *babione* for fearing to touch Angelica:

> Campata avendo Angelica la bella,
> Troppo era lieto di quella aventura.
> Via caminando assai con lei favella,
> Ma di toccarla mai non se assicura.
> Cotanto amava lui quella donzella,
> Che di farla turbare avea paura;
> Turpin, che mai non mente, de ragione
> In cotale atto il chiama un babione.
>
> (II.19.50)

The true test of Orlando's masculinity comes, for Chimenz, when Orlando finds himself alone with Angelica and shows no physical reaction to her caresses. Angelica, in order to solicit Orlando's aid in defending her castle at Albraca, receives him with kisses, embraces and a bath. Despite the fondling attention of the lady he loves, Orlando, though pleased, does not respond as a lover might be expected to respond:

> Stavasi 'l conte quieto e vergognoso,
> Mentre la dama intorno il maneggiava;
> E benché fosse di questo gioioso,
> Crescere in alcun loco non mostrava.

> Intra nel fine in quel bagno odoroso,
> E sé dal collo in giù tutto lavava
> E poi che asciutto fu, con gran diletto
> Per poco spazio se colca nel letto.
> (I.25.39)

Chimenz' notion that Orlando is physically incapable of response is contradicted when later Angelica awakens him and he, trembling as always, embraces her; he regards this reaction, however, as an error and asks Angelica's forgiveness (I.27.49-53). When the Count is roused from sleep, in the dullness of the first waking moments, he momentarily loses the self-restraint, the *mezura*, which is essential to the perpetuation of his pure love, and almost involuntarily oversteps the bounds of propriety by embracing Angelica. The Poet says of his action:

> E la dama abracciò tutto tremando,
> *Benché* soletti fussero in quel loco.
> (I.27.50)

The comment can be read to mean that he *trembled* even though they were alone or he *embraced* her even though they were alone, or he both trembled and embraced her even though they were alone. Whatever the poet intended, it is clear that the response and the plea for forgiveness could only be those of a *fin' aman*. The medieval knight knew that concupiscence was a natural attribute only of women, and that while the state of being in love was acceptable, the *act* of love had no place in the relationship between *fin' aman* and his lady (or any other lady, except, at times, a country girl, a *vilaine*, who was, of course, no lady.) Furthermore, in the courtly tradition we find that what was permitted in public was not permitted in private. It was in private that the true lover was least likely to embrace the lady. What Valency says applies in part to Angelica's behavior:

> The ladies of the *chanson de geste*, in spite of the summary treatment they ordinarily receive, serve their knights indefatigably. They disarm them, bathe them and massage them after their warlike exertions, and often they wait upon them in other ways, less consonant with honor.[15]

---

[15] *Ibid.*, p. 54.

The good knight, the knight with self-control, however, will reject the lady's additional courtesies with "a lesson calculated to improve her morals" or he may even "send her sprawling with a kick in the belly." [16] Orlando's embrace was thus unacceptable especially because they were alone; he was ideal in his behavior only when "crescere in alcun loco non mostrava."

After Orlando's apology each vows to serve the other to the fullest extent, which reminds us that Orlando's love is expressed as just that, service, and little more. That Angelica is falsely imitating the behavior expected of the lady is irrelevant to understanding the relationship. Orlando always remains a combatant knight with a wandering eye, with a touch of the timid, but above all, inexperienced *fin' aman* in him. Orlando's sexual attraction to Origille serves only to emphasize how different his love for Angelica really is. Because Origille is *not* a "lady" his heart is inflamed with desire for her. As for Angelica, he cannot conceive of a fulfillment, in conventional terms, of her promise to reward him with every pleasure possible, even though the idea fascinates him, for that would change his pure love into an impure love, the *amor mixtus* of Andreas. As a *courtly lover* he has already experienced the ultimate delight; the ritual of the bath, the massage and the promise fulfill his every wish:

> Io son venuto nella fin del mondo
> Per l'amor d'una dama conquistare,
> *Et ebbi iesira un giorno sì iocondo,*
> Quanto m'avria saputo imaginare.
> (I.25.54: my italics)

The laws of love to which he is loyal are in fact "opposed to the 'satisfaction' of love, as de Rougemont says, for" 'Whatever turns into a reality is no longer love.' " [17] Hence Orlando, unlike Tristan or Lancelot, never profanes love by actually possessing a woman, for as Turpin claims (I.24.14) he remained virginal and chaste throughout his life. But what of his wife Alda? Unless he really was physically deficient or she was a sort of St. Catherine who

---

[16] *Loc. cit.*
[17] Denis deRougemont, *Love in the Western World*, trans. Montgomery Belgion (New York, 1957), p. 23. The quote is from Claude Fauriel, *Histoire de la poésie provençale* (Paris, 1846), I, p. 512.

took no interest in seeing her marriage consummated, there seems to be an inconsistency. In the eyes of the God of Love, however, there is no inconsistency, for, as Andreas Capellanus would maintain, marriage has nothing to do with love, they are mutually exclusive.

If one were to compare Boiardo's poem to others, perhaps the most favorable comparison which might be made would be one, not between Boiardo and Ariosto, but rather between Boiardo and the troubadours. Of them and their song is said something which can be said of Boiardo and his song of love:

> Nothing is more unlikely, however, than the idea that the characteristically disjunctive quality of the *chanson* was due to some constitutional inability of the troubadours to integrate a logical sequence or to fit it into a rhyme-pattern. The troubadours were virtuosi. No poets in the history of Western literature have demonstrated a surer mastery of their medium. They were certainly capable — as we see from poetic forms other than the love-song — of achieving when they wished a completely unified and consequential expression. The *chanson* was conceived in a different spirit. Like the moods which it expressed, it rejected the dictation of logic in favor of a stream of association, and the *tornada* ended the song only by interrupting it. [18]

That Boiardo too was a virtuoso is confirmed by a reading of his *Amorum libri*.

Up to this point we have considered only the external manifestation of Orlando's love, what is, in a sense, inauthentic about it. Further analysis reveals that the true essence of his love takes the form of a private tragic experience in part because the formulas of the past are insufficient to contain it. Although Orlando's love is steeped in the formalities of tradition, it is more than a generic reflection of the socialized (feudal, hierarchical and vertical) concepts of a crystallized ritual. Between the moment of his departure and the hour of reunion, when the conflict between Love and Honor reaches its most critical point as Orlando must

---

[18] Valency, pp. 139-40.

fight for Charlemagne in order to gain Angelica, the love-struck hero embarks upon an odyssey of love which transforms his desire from a conditioned response to a personal experience. His love becomes a conflict between the stylized idealization of courtly behavior and the internalized agony of a personal compulsion which threatens to destroy his community and all that he as a great warrior has been. Without him the Empire is lost and he, in turn, is destroyed, for Orlando's being is defined, up to the point of his enamorment, by his deeds. The alien power of love, which has no expression in the chivalric code, threatens the *gesta*, the community, the deeds of the hero and the veracity of the chronicle of those deeds.

Domenico De Robertis has said that Boiardo's own love story in his *Canzoniere* reads like literary history: "E l'itinerario sentimentale si dispone infatti, al contrario che per Lorenzo, secondo quello [contenuto] della storia letteraria." [19] If the first book of the *Amorum libri*, he says, corresponds to a "stilnovistic" moment, the second book corresponds to a petrarchan moment, while the third tries to recapture the essence of the Poet's experience through a distillation which expresses a "nuovo gusto". The same might be also said of the *Orlando innamorato*, which, if it is cloaked in a patchwork of inherited conceits, also supercedes its inheritance with a resolution of its own. The question which then arises is to what extent is Orlando the depersonalized figure of a lover caught in the web of the formalized construct of antiquated behavior, and to what extent is his love (his breaking away from his community because of an outside force) an expression of an *individuum*, of the consciousness of subjectivity, and of a passion for which there are no sanctioned guide-lines.

Although some of the traditional rhetoric survives throughout the Poem, the process whereby Orlando's love is transformed begins immediately. The initial moment of love, for example, reflects within itself a synthesis: Orlando is a married courtly lover, but the fact of his marriage becomes instantly insignificant; he is petrarchan because he recognizes his love as an *errore*, but the metaphysical dialectic on which the *errore* is founded withers

---

[19] Domenico De Robertis, "L'esperienza poetica del Quattrocento", in *Storia della letteratura Italiana* (Milan: Garzanti, 1966), III, p. 585.

instantly as God is never mentioned again in connection with Orlando's love, just as Alda, his wife, ceases to exist at all after she is once mentioned. In addition, he falls victim to love because of pride, which, as a restatement of the arrogance which caused Apollo to become the victim of Cupid's revenge, suggests a Humanist's neo-petrarchan addition to the process of enamorment.

Against the background of tradition Orlando's love becomes a fulfillment of Italian personalism at the expense of a feudal hierarchical collectivism. Although early Italian love poetry has its roots in the high feudal value system of Provence, the essentially urban and non-feudal Italian milieu caused the poets of love in Italy to emphasize the private function of love at the expense of the public. Only the Italian poet dared to *name* his lady and then admit to an unmediated relationship in which the adoration of the lady originated in the heart of the poet rather than in the being of the other (the *gilos*). The apogee of this personalism is reached in Dante's relationship with Beatrice, source of his personal salvation, and in the poetry of Petrarch, in which Laura is transformed into an adornment on the monument of the Poet erected in veneration of his own Self. The emotions of the Italian lover are so intense that the traditional restraint which was essential to the preservation of the feudal love of Provence deteriorates and the poet loses control of his passions. The loss of control takes the form, not of an assault upon the lady, but of a disruption of the mind. As Guido delle Colonne says:

> Amor fa disviare li più saggi:
> e chi più ama men' ha in sé misura,
> più folle è quello che più s'innamora. [20]

---

[20] The text quoted is from *Poeti del Duecento*, ed. Gianfranco Contini (Milan, 1960), Vol. I, p. 106. It should be noted, at this point, that Dante is for the most part atypical on the subject of Love's effect on the mind, and declares in the *Vita Nuova*, for example, that Beatrice's image was so pure "che nulla volta sofferse che Amor mi reggesse sanza lo fedele consiglio de la ragione." (The citation is to Michele Barbi's critical edition, Florence: Bemporad, 1932, pp. 9-10.) However, when he writes concerning the *gentile donna* to whom he is attracted after the "trapassamento" of Beatrice (Canzone seconda, *Convivio*, ed. G. Busnelli and G. Vandelli, Florence, 1964) he says:

> Amor che ne la mente mi ragiona
> de la mia donna disiosamente
> move cose de lei meco sovente,
> che lo 'ntelletto sovr'esse disvia.

and Guido Cavalcanti adds:

> Amor mi sforza,
> Contra cui no val forza — ni mesura. [21]

In the end, when all *mesura* is lost, the lover becomes first an autistic psycopath — indifferent to his community's needs, like Orlando *innamorato* — and then a lunatic, like Orlando *furioso*, but above all the lover is struggling not with love but with his own love, with little thought to its sociological significance. As Maurice Valency says of the *stilnovisti's* poetry:

> The poetry of the *stilnovisti* was not public poetry like that of the troubadours; it was infinitely more exclusive, and it was unnecessary in the poetry of so private a nature to promote a purely social ideal. [22]

The very naming of the lady, furthermore, altered the relationship between the lover and his lady; it removes one of two vertical supports, one physical, the other metaphysical, of the notion of love, and places the lover and his lady in a horizontal (temporal and finite) relationship. The lady descends into human time and space and becomes exposed to the ultimate human experience which is death. (The theme of death has occurred earlier, as in the poetry of Giacomino Pugliese, but love of the unnamed lady did not survive much beyond her own demise.) The spiritual relationship between the lady and her admirer, however, remains vertical and ultimately metaphysical; the lady is the exemplar of human virtue, but of absolute virtue, and therefore, she is a morally superior source of admiration to the poet. In the case of Angelica, the second vertical support is removed (the notion of opposition

---

The history of the effects of Love on the mind is of course quite lengthy and beyond the scope of this endeavor. Among the more common sources of the idea of love as madness, as already noted by Durling, are Horace, Chretien de Troyes and the Tristan legend. In addition there is the *fol' amors* which Provençal poets classed apart from *fin' amors*.

[21] Quoted by Valency, p. 234. Cf. Petrarch: Canzoni 125 and 264; Sonnet 236.

[22] *Loc. cit.* Again Dante must be granted a special dispensation for while the poetry of the *stilnovisti* may lose its "social" dimension, with Dante, at least, it retains a "public" dimension by virtue of the theological background against which the poet's love is developed. See C. S. Singleton, *An Essay of the Vita Nuova* (Cambridge, Mass., 1958), pp. 55-77.

between love of God and love of worldly objects is absent, as is the suggestion of a moral *askesis*) and the relationship between her and Orlando becomes fully horizontal. She becomes not only mortal but spiritually corruptible and susceptible to a moral inconsistency which may even make her unworthy of her suitor's fidelity and devotion. The opposition between God and the world is then transformed into an opposition between Society and the Self. Meanwhile, Orlando is of course unaware of his lady's deficiencies, just as Don Quixote, the Spanish reincarnation of Orlando, is unaware of Dulcinea's humble nature. Thus there is irony in the name of Angelica, for she is not the *donna-angelicata* who, like Guido Guinicelli's lady, is analogous to the Angels, whose function it is to carry into effect the thought of God in creation. If anything, Angelica's function is to contradict God's thought.

But the real crisis of the *Innamorato* is not the hero's wandering from God; rather it is his wandering from the world, from the community into a world of fantasy and personal gratification. Orlando implicitly becomes the prefiguration of the "être problématique" who is alienated by an "opposition radicale entre l'homme et le monde, entre l'homme et la société."[23] This occurs when Orlando's love changes and becomes a threat to society, when it ceases to be public (everyone, including the King was enchanted by Angelica) and becomes a private venture, when the quest for Angelica ceases to be a tournament with Angelica as reward and becomes a journey into the territory of the *outsider*, into an unknown foreign environment.

When Orlando the paladin of Charlemagne is transformed into a knight errant guided by his own desires he becomes first a stranger and then a threat to his community. As a sign of his isolation and freedom, perhaps, Orlando puts asides the dress which identified him in the community and, upon his departure, puts on the vestments of personal passion:

> Già non portò la insegna del quartero,
> Ma de un vermiglio scuro era vestito.
> (I.2.28)

---

[23] Lucien Goldman, "Introduction aux premiers écrits de Georges Lukacs," in *Théorie du roman*, cited above, p. 171.

There would appear to be some symbolic significance in the fact that when he returns he is wearing his old "scudo e sopraveste de quartiero" which is "divisato bianco e di vermiglio" (II.29.41). Then when he becomes again a defender of Charlemagne in order to win Angelica, the blood of battle (II.31.27) turns his red and white armor almost all red, as a suggestion, it would seem, that Love is his true motivation.

The realization that Love rather than Honor is his true motivation is forced upon Orlando midway in his quest of Angelica when Dudone, who was sent by Charlemagne to find Ranaldo and Orlando, reports to them that Agramante is about to attack France. When Ranaldo hears this he immediately, instinctively almost, knows he must return to aid his king. Orlando, on the other hand, is caught in a moral crisis which finds him unable to chose between public duty and private fulfillment:

> Ranaldo incontinente se dispose
> Senza altra indugia in Francia ritornare.
> Il conte a quel parlar nulla rispose,
> Stando sospeso e tacito a pensare,
> Ché il core ardente e le voglie amorose
> Nol lasciavan se stesso governare;
> L'amor, l'onor, il debito e 'l diletto
> Facean battaglia dentro dal suo petto.
>
> Ben lo stringeva il debito e l'onore
> De ritrovarse alla reale impresa;
> E tanto più ch'egli era senatore
> E campïon della Romana Chiesa.
> Ma quel che vince ogni omo, io dico Amore,
> Gli avea di tal furor l'anima accesa,
> Che stimava ogni cosa una vil fronda,
> Fuor che vedere Angelica la bionda.
>   (II.9.46-47)

Because Love, which causes him to esteem everything other than seeing Angelica "una vil fronda," conquers Orlando as it does everyone, he abandons his companions:

> Né dir sapria che scusa ritrovasse,
> Ma da' compagni si fu dispartito.
>   (II.9.48)

At this point the Poet abandons Orlando; when he returns to him we learn that Orlando is truly obsessed with thoughts of his lady:

> Però che mi conviene ora tornare
> Al conte Orlando, qual, come io contai,
> Volse questi compagni abandonare,
> Sol per colei che gli dona tal guai,
> Che giorni e notte nol lascia posare;
> E quel pensier non l'abandona mai,
> Ma sempre a rivederla lo retira:
> Sol di lei pensa e sol per lei sospira.
> (II.10.55)

The single-minded lover grants Charlemagne neither a thought not a sigh.

Earlier (I.25) love had alienated Orlando from his own cousin, Ranaldo, who, as one who hates Angelica, might well represent the community and the chivalric code which Orlando, through love, rejects. The difference between the old value system and the new-found individualistic values of Orlando are reflected to some extent in the difference between Ranaldo's emotional response and Orlando's. Ranaldo is the victim of an external force which causes him to hate Angelica, and his behavior is justified by his inability to act freely, humanistically. Orlando, on the other hand, is fully aware of the nature and consequences of his responses and deals with his experience as a personal struggle. He knows "Ché compagnia non vôle amor né stato" (I.25.56). No accommodation can be reached between private desire and public *debito*, when the latter impedes the development of the former. Because he is guided by the irrational power of love Orlando decides he will fight Ranaldo and, thereby, violate the nearly sacred bonds established by their ancestors, even though he knows he is acting irrationally:

> Ché! dico io, adunque fia abattuta
> La lunga parentezza ed amistade,
> Che fu da' nostri antiqui mantenuta?
> Mal faccio, e lo cognosco in veritade;
> Ma da dritta ragione amor mi muta,
> E fia partita al tutto con le spade
> Nostra amistade antiqua e parentella,
> E l'amor nostro di questa donzella.
> (I.25.58)

The repetition of words which are the heart of collective values underscores the monumental significance of Orlando's rejection of them — *nostri antiqui, Nostra amistade antiqua, amistade, parentezza, parentella,* all the time-honored bonds which contribute to the solidarity and stability of a community. But Orlando is an unstable wanderer. The theme of madness, which reaches its peak in the *Furioso*, has attained the level of a *disviare*, to use Guido delle Colonne's word, the wandering from the path of *dritta ragione*. Orlando, like Petrarch, is still aware of his *errore* at this point.

There is the suggestion in the *Innamorato* that Orlando's conscious abandonment of reason is characteristic not only of lovers but of all men who are driven by "Desio di chiara fama, isdegno e amore" for as the inscription above the gate which leads to the Fount of Laughter says:

> 'Amore, isdegno e il desiare onore
> Quando hanno preso l'animo in balìa,
> Lo sospingon avanti a tal fracasso,
> Che poi non trova a ritornar il passo.'
> (III.7.13)

Most passions, however, stop far short of the tragic isolation in which the individual loses all possibility of achieving an "adéquation de l'âme et du monde, de l'intérieur et de l'extérieur."[24] In fact, only Orlando and Rodamonte are possessed by a passionate obsession so great that they become totally irresponsible and completely indifferent to societal limitations. Rodamonte, who declares himself his own God ("sono il mio dio" II.3.22), madly leads his people toward an assault on France in the face of a prophecy that most will die. For himself he does not care whether he arrives in France dead or alive (II.6.10), for even dead he believes he would be invincible.

Even if it were true, as Durling says, with reference to the *Furioso*, that "The madness of Orlando is simply the extreme form of what is universal" it is less true, as he adds, for Boiardo at least, that "La pazzia è tutt'una."[25] There are at least two forms

---

[24] *Loc. cit.* Lukacs sees the epic as an expression of such an "adéquation".
[25] Durling, p. 165.

of madness, one is the rational *temporary* insanity of Sacripante, who finally chooses duty over love, for he knows that the destruction of his people, which is occurring while he is away in search of Angelica, is happening "Contra a ragione" (II.3.12), and *ragione* is his ultimate guide. The other madness is the irrational autism of Orlando and Rodamonte, which acts as a positive danger to their respective societies.

Orlando's love becomes such an active force of opposition when he returns to France and is offered Angelica, who is then in the French camp, as a reward for aiding Charlemagne. Knowing that he can only win Angelica by serving his King he prays God that Charlemagne may be defeated so that he (Orlando) might come to the King's rescue and be personally responsible for the salvation of France:

> Venne in quel bosco e scese Brigliadoro,
> E là pregava Iddio devotamente
> Che le sante bandiere a zigli d'oro
> Siano abattute e Carlo e la sua gente.
> (II.30.61)

As Angelica herself would say (I.3.48): "Ma dove è amor, ragion non trova loco."

The metamorphosis from Roland, who would sacrifice the self for society, to Orlando, who would elevate private fulfillment above public obligation, reflects, it seems, the concern induced by a transition from a feudal to a more humanistic concept of man. Through his prayer Orlando is transformed from a vassal, a mechanism of war, into a sort of *homo sibi relictus*, a man of *virtù* and master of his own destiny who has a "concezione del vivere tutta incentra nel concetto di umanità come libertà, pensosa dell'interiorità ove l'uomo celebra veramente sè stesso." [26] It was Boiardo's cousin, Pico della Mirandola, who said:

> O supreme generosity of God the Father, O highest and most marvelous felicity of man To him it is granted to have whatever he chooses, to be whatever he wills. [27]

---

[26] Eugenio Garin, *Il rinascimento italiano* (Milan, 1941), p. 7.
[27] Pico della Mirandola, "Oration of the Dignity of Man", trans. P. O. Kristeller, in *The Renaissance Philosophy of Man,* eds. E. Cassirer, P. O. Kristeller, J. H. Randall, Jr. (Chicago, 1961), p. 225.

What the Humanists themselves had in mind, as has been shown especially by Professor Garin, was not, however, the type of romantic individualism which Burkhardt detected in the Renaissance spirit, but rather a spirit of self-fulfillment which would be both a glorification of human liberty and a contribution to a more dignified *social* existence. As a sociological document the *Orlando innamorato* bears witness to a crisis of values created by the shift from a society in which a man functions according to the needs of the state and a society wherein the state might ideally function according to the needs of man. Because Boiardo in the end did choose to reconcile to some extent the conflict between love and honor, between the private and the public realms, we cannot interpret his poem merely as a condemnation of the new individualism, or personalism, which threatened the ethical and moral standards of the chivalric code. Rather we are inclined to see it as a literature of transition from one world to another, from a world as it is defined in the chronicle of Turoldus or of Turpin to a world in which the concept of "courtliness" is expanded. Orlando is caught between two sets of values and is forced to reject one (Honor) not *per se*, but because the two are, in his experience, mutually exclusive. With a redefinition of the court comes the fusion of aristocratic, bourgeois and intellectual aspirations, which takes the form of a courtly Humanism as flourished in Ferrara. As Mengaldo says:

> Sembra che si possa obiettivamente parlare di un processo di provincializzazionè dell'umanesimo ferrareso dopo Guarino, e del passaggio da un umanesimo scientifico, più rigoroso e insieme aperto, a un umanesimo 'di corte', ...La corte esercita sulla cultura ferrarese del secondo '400 una funzione così determinante quale non è forse possibile ritrovare in nessun altro centro politico-culturale italiano dell'epoca.[28]

The Humanists gravitate, as a class unto themselves, toward the well-situated because of economic dependence, as von Martin points out.[29] At the same time class alliances are expanding as

---

[28] Pier Vincenzo Mengaldo, *La lingua del Boiardo lirico* (Florence, 1963), pp. 4-5.
[29] Alfred von Martin, *Sociology of the Renaissance* (New York, 1963), p. 46.

aristocrats become capitalists and the bourgeois acquire aristocratic states and becomes attached to courts in the capacity of functionaries. "Even the republican city states," as von Martin says, "had from the beginning harboured the germs of this aristocratization of the *haute bourgeoisie*." [30] The same historian, in describing the relationship between aristocracy and bourgeoisie in Boiardo's period goes on to say:

> By its very nature a court can never dispense with an aristocracy, it can never be composed of bourgeois elements representative of money capital and the intelligentsia. So in the fifteenth and sixteenth centuries the court influence brought about a revival of the nobility.... At the same time the converse already obtained; the outlook of the nobility was exerting an increasing influence upon the bourgeoisie. [31]

This suggests that Boiardo's audience is probably a more loosely defined court society than its medieval predecessors, and it is perhaps for this reason that the Poet transforms the *Signori* and *cavallieri* of the early cantos of the Poem into *Amanti* who are noble not by birth, necessarily, but by virtue of their acquired gentility. It allows the likes of a successful bourgeois *entrepreneur* such as Filippo di Matteo Strozzi, the founder of a family fortune, and a man of considerable importance in the court of Ferdinand I of Naples,[32] to be defined as a courtier. In the case of Giuliano Gondi, whose career closely parallels that of Filippo, the definition was, in fact, official, for "either Ferdinand or his successor granted Giuliano and his heirs the right to incorporate a ducal crown into their coat of arms." [33] The example of Giuliano Gondi is interesting in our context because he was, in Boiardo's lifetime, ambassador to Ferrara and a creditor of Ercole d'Este, which latter fact made him a man who had "personal influence with the Duke." [34] As an established feudal lord Boiardo may have been dismayed by this revolutionary process, while as a semi-noble bourgeois Ariosto was most probably amused by it.

---

[30] *Ibid.*, p. 70.
[31] *Ibid.*, p. 74.
[32] Richard A. Goldthwaite, *Private Wealth in Renaissance Florence: a Study of Four Families* (Princeton, 1968), pp. 52-56.
[33] *Ibid.*, p. 161n.
[34] *Ibid.*, p. 163.

Chapter Three

THE MEANING OF NOBILITY

The Boiardi, along with the Counts of Correggio and the Houses of Pio da Carpi and Pico della Mirandola, were prominent among those who comprised the courtly society which surrounded the Este family in the fifteenth century.[1] In 1362 Selvatico and Feltrino Boiardi were made feudal lords of Rubiera by the Marchese Niccolò II d'Este and the Boiardi held that position until 1423. At that time Feltrino Boiardo the younger ceded the lordship of Rubiera to Niccolò III in exchange for the title of Count of Scandiano and feudal lord of other smaller towns.[2] Later, in 1449, Borso d'Este granted to Feltrino the fief of Salvaterra, which had been ceded to Borso by his brother Leonello.[3] In 1453 Borso renewed Feltrino's investiture and added to his domains Casalgrande, Dinazzano and Montebabbio.[4] Thus it is clear that the Boiardi were liked and well cared for by the Este family.

As for Matteo Boiardo himself, we know that he spent most of the first ten years of his life at the Court of the cultured

---

[1] Edmund G. Gardner, *Dukes and Poets in Ferrara* (London, 1904), p. 18.
[2] Niccolò was actually responsible for making Feltrino feudal lord of Scandiano and the other towns. The title of Count was granted upon request by the Duke of Milan in a declaration issued on the 13th of December, 1423, which made Scandiano independent of Reggio (which had been sold to the Visconti of Milan by the Gonzagas in 1371) and Feltrino's male heirs the legitimate Counts of that locale. See Zottoli's Introduction to *Tutte le opere di M.M.B.* cited above, p. XXXIX.
[3] *Loc. cit.*
[4] *Op. cit.*, p. XL.

Leonello, was later well liked by Borso, the first Duke of Ferrara, and that he was a devoted and intimate companion of Ercole, who succeeded Borso in 1471. It is not surprising, therefore, that Matteo Maria would compose a number of *Carmina* praising the Este, or that he would return to praising them in the *Orlando innamorato*. The Poet knew of course that, although the Este family was one of the most illustrious of Italian noble families, tracing its history nearly as far back as the carolingian era, it could use some encomiastic exaltation to dispel the rumor that they were descended from the infamously treacherous Count Guenelon, the stepfather of Roland who conspired with the Saracen King Marsilion to destroy Roland.[5] In addition the memory lingered of Obizzo II (1247-1293), the fourth Este lord of Ferrara, who was found by Dante among the violent souls in a river of blood in the seventh circle of Hell (Inferno XII), as lingered also the memory of Azzo VIII, to whom Jacopo del Cassero in *Purgatory* (Canto V) attributes his murder.[6]

Although Boiardo's fondness for the Este family is understandable, his decision in the *Orlando innamorato* to have the future establishment of the House of Este depend upon the ability of a thief to steal a ring might seem less comprehensible. This, however, is precisely what happens. Boiardo certainly did not intend in any way to disparage the names of Ercole d'Este and his legendary ancestor, Ruggiero. On the contrary, a careful reading of the Brunello episode reveals that the constant association between Ruggiero and the thief Brunello serves only to brighten the name of Ruggiero, and by inference, that of Ercole. The story of Brunello, who through his skill becomes a king, also raises the question of the meaning of nobility as it is understood within the limits of the poetic microcosm, and, possibly, as it may have presented itself to the noble author in the context of the aristocratic reality of his everyday world. Unfortunately historical scholarship has provided only a vague outline of the

---

[5] Apparently the rumor was started in Padova. See M. M. Boiardo, *Orlando Innamorato, Amorum Libri*, ed. Aldo Scaglione, cited above, II, pp. 9-10n.

[6] Later Benvenuto da Imola was to mollify somewhat the judgments of the *Divine Comedy* by dedicating his commentary on that work to Niccolò II d'Este, as Gardner points out (*Op. cit.*, p. 17).

historical situation in Ferrara during Boiardo's life-time. What influence the new financial-mercantile class had on the nobility, what the position of the intellectual "nobility" was, are for example, the type of questions which must be answered before we can make a positive statement on a direct correspondence between the values reflected in the Poem and those which may have prevailed in the society in which the author was a prominent figure. For this reason, any comparisons made between the world of the Poem and Ferrara in the Quattrocento can only be assigned the value of inference and suggestion. The mere fact that Boiardo questions the meaning of nobility in the Poem is proof, at least, that certain aristocratic concepts were not entirely static in the mind of the author. Within the limits of the Poem we find that certain values, which can be related to the structure of the work itself (as in the metamorphosis of the audience), are not accepted without challenge.

In the opening canto of Book Two, Agramante, a descendant of Alexander and king of the Saracens, decides to invade France. With that notion in mind he calls his vassals together to consider his plan. While the older leaders at that meeting urge caution, the brash Rodamonte, King of Sarza, accuses them of cowardice and lack of sense (II.1.53). Rodamonte, who is still *acerbo* (II.1. 56), or unripened by experience, is eager to rush into battle, despite the warning of the Astrologer-King of Garamanta, who declares that their venture is destined to fail. The Astrologer warns that all will be killed and that even Rodamonte "con sua gran possanza / Diverrà pasto de' corbi de Franza" (II.1.59). Agramante and Rodamonte, however, are still determined to wage war against Charlemagne. Rodamonte rejects the prophecy and says he will be his own prophet:

    —Mentre che siam qua, — disse — io son contento
    Che quivi profetezi a tuo talento;

    Ma quando tutti avrem passato il mare,
    E Franza struggeremo a ferro e a foco,
    Non me venistù intorno a indovinare,
    Perch'io serò il profeta di quel loco.
    Male a quest'altri pôi ben minacciare,

> A me non già, che ti credo assai poco,
> Perché scemo cervello e molto vino
> Parla te fa da parte de Apollino. —
>   (II.1.60-61)

When the King of Garamanta finally agrees to join them in their campaign, he asks only one concession, namely that they not go without Ruggiero, "Fiore e corona de ogni cavalliero" (II.1.71), who is their only hope of success. The King informs Agramante that Ruggiero is in the care of the astrologer and magician Atlas, who has hidden him in a magic garden on Mount Carena because he knows that betrayal and a violent death await him in France. With this a search for Ruggiero begins only to end in failure, as we learn in the third canto. Rodamonte, meanwhile, is anxious to sail for France and believes the story of an enchanted garden to be a deception intended to delay the war. The Astrologer-King of Garamanta in turn declares Rodamonte insane (II.3.28) and states that the garden can be disenchanted and Ruggiero found with the aid of Angelica's ring, which renders every enchantment ineffective:

> Io so che Rodamonte ciò non crede:
> Mirati come ride quell'insano!
> Ma se uno annel ch'io sazo, pôi avere,
> Questo giardino ancor potrai vedere.
>
>   L'annello è fabricato a tal ragione
> (Come più volte è già fatto la prova)
> Che ogni opra finta de incantazione
> Convien che a sua presenzia se rimova.
> Questo ha la figlia del re Galafrone,
> Qual nel presente in India se ritrova,
> Presso al Cataio, intra un girone adorno,
> Ed ha l'assedio di Marfisa intorno.
>
>   Se questo annello in possanza non hai,
> Indarno quel giardin se può cercare,
> Ma sii ben certo non trovarlo mai.
>   (II.3.28-30)

He concludes, shortly thereafter, by forecasting his own death:

> Poi che ebbe il vecchio re così parlato
> Chinò la faccia lacrimando forte.

> — Più son — dicea — de gli altri sventurato,
> Ché cognosco anzi il tempo la mia sorte;
> Per vera prova di quel che ho contato,
> Dico che gionta adesso è la mia morte:
> Come il sol entra in cancro a ponto a ponto,
> Al fine è il tempo di mia vita gionto.
> (II.3.31)

Having decided that Ruggiero must be found, Agramante announces (II.3.38) that whoever is successful in stealing Angelica's ring will be made king of many regions and given a vast treasure. The King of Fiessa, upon hearing this, decides that he would like to offer the services of his servant Brunello, who is an extraordinary thief. At this point the fates of Ruggiero and Brunello begin to become strangely intertwined. If Brunello succeeds in stealing the ring he will make himself a king and will prepare the way for a chain of events which will eventually lead to the marriage of Ruggiero and Bradamante and the founding of the House of Este. Both Brunello and Ruggiero appear almost as if by magic; Ruggiero from an enchanted garden and Brunello from the unknown depths of servitude. Both are destined to achieve great social status. Yet there is a difference. No one would deny that Ruggiero deserves an honorable place in society, for he is Agramante's cousin (II.1.70). Brunello seems less acceptable as a nobleman, not only because he is of humble origin, but because of his ignoble ambition. He does not accept the challenge of stealing the magic ring because of the honor it will bring him but because of the status he will gain. His first self-confident words are not that he will succeed in getting the ring but that he will succeed in acquiring a kingdom:

> Disse: — Segnore, io non posserò mai,
> Sin che con l'arte, inganni, o con ingegno
> Io non acquisti il promettuto regno.
> (II.3.41)

Brunello does succeed in getting Angelica's ring (II.5.34) and on his way back he also steals Sacripante's horse (II.5.40), Marfisa's sword (II.5.41) and Orlando's sword and horn (II.11.7-9). When he delivers the ring to Agramante he is crowned King of Tingitana:

> Il re Agramante in piede fo levato,
> E in presenzia di tutti a mano a mano
> Ebbe Brunello il ladro incoronato,
> Donando a lui de Tingitana il regno,
> Populi e terre ed ogni suo contegno.
>
> (II.16.14)

From the moment he utters his first words Brunello is portrayed as what in Boiardo's day would have been called a *novus homo*, "an upstart" resembling perhaps Giovanni di Bicci de' Medici, who "was looked down on by the possessors of older wealth."[7] As a King he is nothing but a *nouveau riche* member of a newly emerging class completely lacking, as far as the established aristocracy is concerned, in nobility of character.

When Ruggiero is finally drawn out of the garden by a clever plan of Brunello, he borrows Brunello's arms in order to engage in the mock battle which is part of Brunello's plan. (Ruggiero of course thinks the battle is genuine.) To add to the irony inherent in the fact that the flower of chivalry must borrow the arms of a *parvenu*, Ruggiero is mistaken for Brunello by the other Saracen kings, including Agramante, who is shocked to discover that Brunello possesses any *valore*, the one chivalric virtue which would distinguish him as a true nobleman:

> Dicea Agramante: — A Dio mi racomando,
> Ch'io non credetti mai che quel Brunello
> Un regno meritasse per valore:
> Ma ben serebbe degno imperatore. —
>
> (II.17.23)

Later, when Brunello himself returns wearing his blood-stained armor, he is accused of having killed Bardulasto and is condemned to death. He protests and tries to explain that it was Ruggiero who had engaged them in battle wearing his (Brunello's) armor, but the others do not believe him, for they know what a liar he is. They call him an uncouth *grossero* when he unsuccessfully appeals to them by reminding them of his service to the court:

> Onde esso, che se trova in mal pensero,
> Del re e de gli altri se doleva forte,

---

[7] Ferdinand Schevill, *The Medici* (New York, 1960), p. 58.

> Narrando come era ito messagero
> Per quello annello a risco de la morte.
> Gli altri ridendo il chiamano grossero,
> Poi che servigi ramentava in corte;
> Però che ogni servire in cortesano
> La sera è grato e la matina è vano.
> (II.21.37)

Brunello is thus reminded of his lowly position before becoming a king, and the Poet adds a comment the tone of which is difficult to interpret, saying that such is the fate of a courtier, his services are quickly forgotten. Since the others believe that Brunello had unjustly killed Bardulasto the comment cannot be taken merely as a disenchanted denunciation of contemporary courtly and political practices. The following stanza, nevertheless, adds to the suggestion that felicitous relationships can be terminated abruptly, especially if one party becomes too successful or ambitious, for past services were rewarded in the past; sentiment has no exchange value in such strictly practical relationships:

> Proprio è bene un om dal tempo antico
> Chi racordando va quel ch'è passato;
> Ché sempre la risposta è: "Bello amico,
> Stu m'hai servito, ed io te ho ben trattato";
> E per questo Brunel, come io vi dico,
> Era da tutti intorno caleffato,
> E ciascun di lui dice più male,
> Come intraviene a l'om che troppo sale.
> (II.21.38)

Brunello, happily, is rescued by Ruggiero, for he remembers Brunello's services to him; he is presumably superior in courtliness to the others for (II.21.40) "Lui non era di quelli, a non mentire, / Che scordasse il servigio recevuto." Later the name of Brunello is again linked to Ruggiero's, for the latter's request that he be made a *cavaliere* is based on the fact that he defended "la ragione e il dritto" by saving Brunello. When he is beknighted (II.21.52) he is given Brunello's arms and horse, according to his request. Immediately thereafter Atlas foresees the defeat of Charlemagne, the conversion of Ruggiero to Christianity, the death of Ruggiero at the hands of the Maganzesi and the growth of the House of Este.

The constant presence of Brunello evokes various thoughts. He was a king before Ruggiero was made a *cavaliere*, yet Ruggiero is decidedly more aristocratic. The House of Este has an illustrious founder, yet he begins his knighthood with the arms of a thief. The obvious suggestion is that nobility resides not in possessions or acquired titles, but in the inherent superiority of the person. The contrast is between Ruggiero the true aristocrat and Brunello the bourgeois imitator. Elsewhere Brunello in fact reflects a distinctly *nouveau riche* attitude, not unlike that of the middle class citizens of the fifteenth century who were eager to adopt seignorial manners and become aristocrats themselves. In describing his new arms the Poet notes that Brunello's insignia is more conspicuous than most because it is new and probably of audacious design since he designed it himself, just as in modern days people try to improve their family image with *zigli* and *leoni*:

> Dapoi Brunello, il re de Tingitana,
> Avea la insegna di novo ritrata,
> Più vaga assai de l'altre e più soprana,
> Perché lui stesso a suo modo l'ha fatta;
> Come oggi al mondo fa la gente vana,
> Stimando generosa far sua schiatta
> E le casate sue nobile e degne
> Con far de zigli e de leoni insegne.
> (II.29.6)

Like the insecure *gente vana* who have no illustrious family history, Brunello is anxious to prove that his emblem (a goose — *Oca* — on a red field) is an ancient one. He humorously uncovers evidence of this in the fact that the Gospel of St. John says that "Hoc (which Brunello reads as *Oca*) erat in principio."[8] With a pun Brunello shows his contempt for aristocratic genealogy and family history even though he feels obliged to create his own. To some extent he resembles Don Giuliano, a French captain of the bowmen in the army of Charles VIII, who passed through Reggio in August of 1494. In a letter of August 26 to Ercole,

---

[8] John I: 1-2: "In principio erat Verbum, et Verbum erat apud Deum, et Deus erat Verbum. Hoc erat in principio apud Deum."

Boiardo describes the Frenchman as elegantly dressed and wearing many jewels, all of which are false:

> ...Questo homo...era vestito de uno saio di pano biancho cum molte machie di broda, et havea sopra un mantello de veluto nero ornato di balassi e zaffiri e smeraldi e diamanti, stimati assai per Messere: li peci di queste pietre erano setantaquatro, de la grandecia de un carlino o pocho meno, legati benissimo in oro, ma tuti falsi insoma.[9]

Not only his jewels, but his drinking cups and everything else about him are adulterated and false:

> Noi bevemo siecho tuti e tre e facemo bona cira al costume di Franza cum molti napi de argento tuti alchimiati, et di questa sorte è tuto lo aparechio de la credentia sua (al mio parere), la quale m'ha mostrata poi questa matina; et sono molti vasi ben lavorati, parte bianchi e dorati in parte. Li ragionamenti soi sono consimili a questo suo aparato, de qualli potrà Vostra Ex(cellenti)a havere per più bello aggio informatione da Messere.[10]

Brunello, with his eternal emblem, is just as false as Don Giuliano with his seventy-four jewels. Brunello is a status-seeker whose status rests not on genealogical resources but on his personal talents. Unlike other nobles, he is less interested in honor and other such antiquated notions than in protecting his personal interests. When it comes to striving for honor on the battlefield, he is quick to encourage others, but Brunello himself is always last:

> E dietro a tutti stava il re Brunello,
> Benché conforta ogniom che avanti vada,
> Per governar qualcosa che gli cada.
> (II.31.41)

Brunello thus represents the would-be aristocrat who imitates the attitudes of the aristocracy while at the same time posing a threat to the survival of aristocratic class values, for, personally, he lacks the nobility of character which is the mark of a true aristocrat.

---

[9] Mateo Maria Boiardo, *Opere volgari*, ed. Pier Vincenzo Mengaldo (Bari, 1962), p. 297.
[10] *Loc. cit.*

It is another thief, Barigaccio, who argues that, if honor is a vanishing ideal, it is the *gran signori* themselves who are mostly responsible for its disappearance. As a thief he considers himself no worse than the world's leaders, who harm thousands, while he only harms a few:

> Rispose il malandrin: — Questo che io faccio
> Fallo anco al mondo ciascun gran signore;
> E' de' nemici fanno in guerra istraccio
> Per agrandire e far stato maggiore.
> Io solo a sette o dece dono impaccio,
> E loro a dieci millia con furore;
> Tanto ancora di me peggio essi fanno,
> Togliendo quel del che mestier non hanno. —
> (II.19.40)

Brandimarte's ironically compromising reply is one which Barigaccio, who finds rationalizations more offensive than undisguised theft, cannot accept. Barigaccio disagrees with Brandimarte's assertion that the actions of the *gran signori*, because they benefit the state, are pardonable:

> Diceva Brandimarte: — Egli è peccato
> A tuor l'altrui, sì come al mondo se usa;
> Ma pur quando se fa sol per il stato,
> Non è quel male, et è degno di scusa. —
> Rispose il ladro: — Meglio è perdonato
> Quel fallo onde se stesso l'omo accusa;
> Ed io te dico e confessoti a pieno
> Che ciò che io posso, toglio a chi può meno.
> (II.19.41)

By contrast to Barigaccio's straightforwardness, even Brandimarte's character and integrity are shadowed by doubt. He is apparently so accustomed to rationalization that he always feels compelled to justify his actions when taking someone else's property. It so happens that in the episode of Barigaccio, when Brandimarte is attacked by Barigaccio's thieves, Brandimarte is twice constrained by necessity to take what does not belong to him. The first time, when he takes the armor of the dead King Agricane in order to defend himself and Fiordelisa against the thieves, his decision is perfectly justified; the second time, when he takes the horse of the dying Barigaccio, whom he has wounded in a duel, his decision seems less honorable. Brandimarte, after wounding the thief, does not want to administer the *coup de grâce*, and thus leaves him dying on the ground:

> Lui cadde a terra biastemando forte,
> Ed al demonio se racomandava,
> E benché Brandimarte lo conforte,
> Con più nequizia ognior se disperava;
> Ma il cavallier non volse darli morte,
> E così strangosciato lo lasciava,
> Partendosi di qua senza dimora;
> Ma lui moritte appresso in poco d'ora.
> (II.19.46)

Brandimarte left *senza dimora* and Barigaccio died *apresso in poco d'ora*. Then in a sort of flashback the Poet explains that, before leaving, Brandimarte took the *ladrone's* horse:

> Il cavallier, lasciando il ladro fello
> Con la sua dama si volea partire,
> Quando Batoldo, il suo destrier morello,
> Ch'era nel prato, cominciò a nitrire;
> Veggendol Brandimarte tanto bello,
> Con la sua Fiordelisa prese a dire:
> — Il palafren serìa troppo gravato
> Se te portasse e me, che sono armato,
>
> Sì che io me pigliarò quel bon destriero,
> Come pigliato ho il brando e l'armatura,
> Perché serebbe pazzo e mal pensiero
> Lasciar quel che appresenta la ventura.
> Quei morti più de ciò non han mestiero,
> Ché sono usciti fuor de ogni paura. —
> Così dicendo se accosta al ronzone,
> Prendoe la briglia e salta in su lo arcione.
> (II.19.47-48)

Brandimarte's principle reason for taking the *ronzone* is not so much that he needs one, for he was not aware of such a need until he heard the horse neigh. His real reason is that it is foolish to pass up what fortune offers. He even declares Barigaccio dead, and, therefore, in no need of a horse, when we know that he was in fact only wounded.

Brandimarte's treatment of Barigaccio seems more callous than ever when we think of Orlando's reaction after wounding Agricane. We are invited to think back to that great duel by the mention of Agricane's *brando* and *armatura*. It is perhaps no coincidence that the duel between Orlando and Agricane occurred in *canto nineteen* of Book One while that between Brandimarte and Barigaccio takes place in *canto nineteen* of Book Two. Orlando's reaction was one of great sadness as he cried over the wounded king:

> Egli avea pien de lacrime la faccia
> E fo smontato in su la terra piana;
> Ricolse il re ferito nelle braccia,
> E sopra al marmo il pose alla fontana;
> E de pianger con seco non si saccia,
> Chiedendoli perdon con voce umana.
> Poi battizollo a l'acqua della fonte,
> Pregando Dio per lui con le man gionte.
>   (I.19.16)

Of course Barigaccio is not a king and we would not necessarily expect Brandimarte to weep for him. However, we might at least have expected him to offer a prayer for him, especially considering the fact that Barigaccio, unlike Brunello, was a man of remarkable *valore*:

> Il cavallier se maraviglia assai
> Come abbia un malandrin tanta bontade,
> Perché in su vita non vidde più mai
> Tanta fierezza ad altri in veritate.
> Ambi avean l'arme, quale io vi contai;
> Già tutte l'han falsate con le spade,
> Né di ferire alcun di lor se arresta,
> Ma la battaglia cresce a più tempesta.
>   (II.19.35)

So impressed was Brandimarte, in fact, with Barigaccio's *bontade* that he esteemed him a champion and tried to co-opt him by encouraging him to join the ranks of the nobility:

> — Io non so chi tu sia, né per qual modo
> T'abbia condutto a tal mestier fortuna,
> Ma per più prodo campïon te lodo
> Ch'io sappia al mondo, sotto della luna;
> E ben me avedo che fermato è il chiodo,
> Che prima che sia sera o notte bruna,
> O l'uno o l'altro fia nel campo morto;
> E spero che serà colui che ha il torto.

> Ma stu volessi lasciar quel mestiero,
> Qual nel presente fai, di robbatore,
> Vinto mi chiamo e son tuo cavalliero:
> In ogni parte vo' portarti onore.
> Or che farai? Hai tu forse pensiero
> Che manchi giamai robba al tuo valore?
> Lascia questo mestier: non dubitare,
> Ché a tal come sei tu, non può mancare. —
>
> (II.19.38-39)

It is at this point that Barigaccio says, as we have noted, that between him and the heads of state there is little difference.

Implicit in Barigaccio's appraisal is the suggestion that there is an internal threat to the chivalric code and aristocratic values which is posed by the shortcomings of the *segnori e cavallieri* themselves. Brandimarte is somewhat of an opportunist, Orlando is a social misfit, Ranaldo is a "publico ladrone" (I.27.15) and Astolfo is rude (I. 3.28). The only character to possess a nearly exemplary courtly nature is a woman, Bradamante, the sister of Ranaldo and the first of a line of Este women admired for their cultural refinement and sophistication. But even she is far from possessing an absolute sense of fidelity to her King, which fault would seem to be sufficient to disqualify her as an ideal founder of the House of Este. Although she is aware of her obligation to her King, Bradamante, "la dama di valore" (III.5.5), feels she must be primarily dedicated to herself and to the defense of her personal honor. When she first hears from Rodamonte that Charlemagne's forces have been defeated, Bradamante asks Rodamonte that she be allowed to go unimpeded to the aid of her King. Bradamante implores him to grant her wish, for she has no other desire but to die with her King:

> Quando la dama intese così dire,
> Dal fren per doglia abandonò la mano,
> E tutta in faccia se ebbe a scolorire,
> Dicendo a Rodamonte: — Bel germano,
> Questo che io chiedo, non me lo disdire:
> Lascia che io segua il mio segnor soprano,
> Tanto che a quello io me ritrovi apresso,
> Ché il mio volere è di morir con esso.
>
> (III.4.56)

Rodamonte refuses to honor her request and answers it with a challenge to arms. At this point Ruggiero intercedes on behalf of Bradamante, who departs immediately (II.4.59). After having traveled a *bon pezzo*, Bradamante decided that she must return to where she left Ruggiero, for the threat to her honor is more horrible than the threat to Charlemagne:

>   E già bon pezzo essendo caminata,
> Nè potendo sua gente ritrovare,
> La qual fuggiva a briglia abandonata,
> Ne la sua mente se pose a pensare,
> Tra sé dicendo: 'O Bradamante ingrata,
> Ben discortese te puote appellare
> Quel cavallier che non sai chi se sia,
> Ed ha' gli usata tanta villania.
>
>   La zuffa prese lui per mia cagione,
> E le mie spalle il suo petto diffese.
> Ma, se io vedesse quivi il re Carlone
> E le sue gente morte tutte e prese,
> Tornar mi converrebe a quel vallone,
> Sol per vedere il cavallier cortese.
> Sono obligata a l'alto imperatore,
> Ma più sono a me stessa ed al mio onore.'
>   (III.5.6-7)

Bradamante's declaration that she would return to Ruggiero even if the King and his *gente* were before her either dead or captured is nearly as unexpected as Orlando's prayer for the defeat of Charlemagne. When faced with a choice (even a hypothetical choice) between service to society and service to self, Bradamante, like Orlando, chooses to serve the image of the self rather than the needs of society. Her concept of honor is entirely personal; her standard of measure is her own, as must be her notion of what defines the concepts of nobility, *gentilezza* and *cortesia*. By measuring honor on a purely personal scale, Bradamante de-feudalizes it to the extent that, because there is no longer a standard communal measure, it ceases to be a strictly hierarchical value. When each individual has his own idea of honor, it becomes a less exclusive value. At the same time the way is opened to a possible conflict in which the individual may be unable to reconcile his obligation to his community with his obligation to himself.

THE MEANING OF NOBILITY

What the Poet feels about the crisis of values in the Poem is difficult to ascertain, perhaps because he is not certain what to think of it. The one fear which may dominate his social consciousness is that his class (if for a moment we identify the Poet with Boiardo) may not be able to live up to its ideal historical image of itself in the face of a changing social structure which is forcing that class and the meaning of nobility to change. In other words, we might say that the Poet knows that a newly acquired title is no guarantee of courtliness, just as Ruggiero knows that *gentilezza*, nobility of birth, is no guarantee of *cortesia*, nobility of individual personality:

> ... : —Esser non puo ch'io non me doglia,
> Se io trovo gentil omo discortese,
> Però che bene è un ramo senza foglia,
> Fiume senza onda e casa senza via
> La gentilezza senza cortesia.
> (III.4.58)

If to some extent the Poet is fearful that the concept of nobility is threatened both from within and from without, it is also true that he welcomes a re-examination of the standards set for the definition of a *cavaliere*. Through Orlando's conversation with Agricane, the Poet introduces the topos *sapientia et fortitudo* and leads his audience to a reconsideration of courtly ideals.[11] When Orlando pauses to reflect upon the beauty of the universe, Agricane tells him he has never been interested in study and contemplation:

> Disse Agricane: —Io comprendo per certo
> Che tu vôi de la fede ragionare;
> Io de nulla scienza sono esperto,
> Né mai, sendo fanciul, volsi imparare,
> E roppi il capo al mastro mio per merto;
> Poi non si puotè un altro ritrovare
> Che mi mostrasse libro né scrittura,
> Tanto ciascun avea di me paura.
>
> E così spesi la mia fanciulezza
> In caccie, in giochi de arme e in cavalcare;

---

[11] Cf. Curtius, Chapter 9, "Heroes and Rulers", especially Section 6, *Arms and Studies*, pp. 178-9.

> Né mi par che convenga a gentilezza
> Star tutto il giorno ne' libri a pensare;
> Ma la forza del corpo e la destrezza
> Conviense al cavalliero esercitare.
> Dottrina al prete ed al dottor sta bene:
> Io tanto saccio quanto mi conviene.
>   (I.18.42-43)

Orlando counters with a defense of literary culture, stating that it does benefit a knight. He suggests, in fact, that without *sapientia* one would possess neither *cortesia* nor humanity, for he would become like an ox or a stone or a piece of wood:

> Rispose Orlando: —Io tiro teco a un segno,
> Che l'arme son de l'omo il primo onore;
> Ma non già che il saper faccia men degno,
> Anci lo adorna come un prato il fiore;
> Ed è simile a un bove, a un sasso, a un legno,
> Chi non pensa allo eterno Creatore;
> Né ben se può pensar senza dottrina
> La summa maiestate alta e divina. —
>   (I.18.44)

Judging from this exchange we might conclude that, from the point of view of an Italian poet, Orlando's concept of *cortesia* is less French than Agricane's; Orlando seems to have become Italianized even in his ideology. This seems especially true if we recall that not very long after Boiardo's lifetime, letters had become so integral a part of the Italian concept of *cortesia* that Castiglione's Count Ludovico da Canossa remarks that it is the French who do not esteem letters:

> 'But, besides goodness, for everyone the true and principal adornment of the mind is, I think, letters; although the French recognize only the nobility of arms and reckon all the rest as naught; and thus not only do they not esteem, but they abhor letters, and consider all men of letters to be very base; and they think that it is a great insult to call anyone a clerk.' [12]

---

[12] Baldesar Castiglione, *The Book of the Courtier*, trans. Charles S. Singleton (New York, 1959), p. 69.

Giuliano de' Medici adds to this the assertion that "this error has prevailed among the French for a long time now." [13]

Undoubtedly Boiardo's concept of nobility had expanded to include the *dottor* to whom Agricane refers. It is interesting to note that the very title of doctor conveyed, in Boiardo's day as well as in our own, a certain sense of nobility of soul. As Alessandro Visconti points out:

> Bisogna tener presente che il titolo, o meglio, il grado dottorale aveva una grandissima importanza sociale: *doctoratus tribuit nobilitatem*, dice la Glossa. Il dottorato comporta la *licentia docendi*; ed è come una *militia civilis*. E come il cavaliere (*miles*) non poteva essere armato che da un altro cavaliere, così un dottore non poteva essere fatto che da un altro dottore, cioè da un collegio di dottori. Ed è così anche oggi. [14]

But even Moses, Coluccio Salutati believed, had understood nobility to imply erudition:

> Per nobilis ergo quid significavit dux ille sanctissimus, nisi quos prius dixerat gnaros; nisi scientia nisique virtutibus excellentes? [15]

In the final analysis it appears that Boiardo eagerly accepted some changes in the meaning of nobility, such as that permitting the inclusion of literati; tolerated or even embraced others, such as the change reflected in the individualism of Bradamante; and acknowledged others without invective, for Brunello, the new king, is at least portrayed as skillful, clever and confident. The *Innamorato* is devoid of harsh criticism and full of tolerance for human deficiencies. The author's treatment of the aristocracy is not much more generous than his treatment of the less than noble characters.

In real life Boiardo was the generous descendant of a family known for its generosity, and a merciful administrator of justice,

---

[13] *Loc. cit.*

[14] Alessandro Visconti, *La storia dell'Università di Ferrara: 1391-1950* (Bologna, 1950), p. 10.

[15] Coluccio Salutati, *De nobilitate legum et medicinae*, ed. Eugenio Garin (Florence, 1947), p. 10.

whether dealing with ordinary criminals or with the cousin with whom he shared his inheritance, even after the latter conspired to poison him. He was a cultured man who certainly enjoyed the splendors of the Este Court, and whose belief apparently was that the integrity of a society depends upon the integrity of the individuals that constitute that society.

CHAPTER FOUR

TIME, SPACE AND ACTION

Like Astolfo flying to the moon on the hippogriff, Ariosto, by flying on the wings of a liberated imagination, is able to leave the world of Boiardo to find for himself a new point of reference from which to view the action of the chivalric world of his poem. From his new-found *tertium quid* he is able to focus on all the action of the poem all the time. In addition to seeing all, he is able to control all by becoming the controlling demiurge of the poetic microcosm, thus achieving the status of analogue to the Creator of the cosmos.[1] Unlike Ariosto, however, Boiardo is a master among masters, a class equal of Count Orlando, and the perspective from which he views the world of his poem is that of Orlando. He does not often rise above his characters in consciousness; instead, he rides the haunches of his heroes' steeds and sees the world as they see it. That world, for the most part, for both authors, is a communal world of Action and not one of Situations, a world in which solutions are predetermined and not dependent upon a subjective interpretation of the individual. The personality of the individual is defined by his actions and his actions are generally the expression of the ethos of his community. Only the actions of Orlando and Bradamante are in any sense qualitatively different.

Boiardo experiences the life of the Poem as Orlando does, episodically, moment by moment, leaving all that is not directly before him suspended in a state of static preservation. While he

---

[1] Cf. Durling, pp. 126, 132.

rushes over continents with his characters, Boiardo is able to live the experiences of the characters, and, as Ugo Foscolo said, share the joys and sufferings with them individually while forgetting all else. Ariosto, on the other hand, by transporting himself beyond the bounds of his characters' world, is in a position to analyse the life of that world in its relationship to the cosmos which it reflects. His task is to give rational intelligibility to a world which for Boiardo was a succession of spontaneous apparitions quickly forgotten. Thus, as Foscolo noted, Ariosto, unlike Boiardo, is an omniscient master of his poem:

> Quando l'Ariosto mette in campo un suo personaggio, egli non lascia perciò di tener l'occhio sul resto, e sempre ricordasi dell'effetto generale del suo poema. Ma il Boiardo al contrario più s'occupa del tratteggiar l'individuo: egli partecipa delle sue gioie e de' suoi dolori; oblia tutti gli altri, oblia lo stesso lettore. [2]

The difference between the two microcosms, as the titles of the poems suggest, is that Boiardo's is a world of the heart and Ariosto's is a world of the mind; and by making his poem a *"lucid interval* of mind in the rush of the universal madness," [3] Ariosto becomes, not the traveling companion of Orlando that Boiardo is, but "the Providence of the little world of the poem." [4]

Although both Boiardo's and Ariosto's poetic worlds are closed, infinite totalities which are never threatened by the expiration of time, the view each has of the poetic microcosm is radically different from that of the other. While Ariosto's Poet sees his creation from the *tertium quid* of his artistic heaven, or at least from the perspective of the moon, as an indivisible totality *in actu permanente, in facto*, Boiardo's Poet sees, instead of a "simultaneously existing whole," [5] (a possibility Aristotle denied to any form of infinity), a more traditional infinite world which exists *in fieri, successive*, and which is infinite by virtue of its infinite divisibility. If the poet's Song is a whole universe in itself and the

---

[2] Ugo Foscolo, *Opere edite e postume*, Vol. X: *Saggi di critica storico-letteraria* (Florence, 1859), p. 180.
[3] Durling, p. 176.
[4] *Ibid.*, p. 130.
[5] W. D. Ross, *Aristotle*, cited above, pp. 86-87.

greater Universe is a harmonious song, the polyphonic analysis of the musical microcosm is more medieval in Boiardo's poem, stressing each individual voice and each syllable (which syllables "are the successive moments of time.")[6] Ariosto's Song, on the other hand, is distinctly more modern in its emphasis. The difference is that noted by Spitzer between medieval and Renaissance polyphony:

> The new *a Cappella* singing of the fifteenth century is a development from the *rondeau* and canon: four voices enter one after the other, each imitating the preceding one. By now it is simultaneous, not successive, apperception which prevails; this is the very time of the Renaissance when perspective and space are introduced into painting, so that the beholder of the painting must take in simultaneously the depicted figure, and the space around it (which had been absent from medieval painting); now composer and painter alike compose vertically (not horizontally), two dimensionally (not linearly). In medieval polyphony the development had always to be from individual to individual, never was there a supravocal principle: There could be unisons or parallelisms, never the fusion of the particular (linear) voices in a totality.[7]

The difference between the world of the *Orlando innamorato* and the *Orlando furioso* is that which Arnold Hauser finds as

---

[6] Durling, p. 123.

[7] Leo Spitzer, *Classical and Christian Ideas of World Harmony*, ed. Anna Granville Hatcher (Baltimore, 1963), pp. 43-44. We have lost some degree of familiarity with, and reliance upon, the use of analogy, but for centuries it was an integral part of the intellective process. Cassirer, for example, speaks of "...that basic tendency of medieval thought which tries to capture the whole physical and spiritual world in the network of these analogies" (Ernst Cassirer, *The Individual and the Cosmos in Renaissance Philosophy*, trans. Mario Domandi, New York, 1963, p. 88.) In the sixteenth century, as John Shearman notes, analogy was still an important principle: "...our distrust of analogies was not shared by the sixteenth century, which inherited from antiquity a habit of drawing parallels as a matter of course" (John Shearman, *Mannerism*, Baltimore, 1967, p. 32.) Again Cassirer states (p. 149) that "even *Telesio's* theory of knowledge seeks to demonstrate the unity of the intellect and senses by letting all the functions of thought and of 'rational' deduction be rooted in the *single* function of drawing analogies." It is with this in mind that the explanation by analogy is here introduced.

an element which distinguishes Gothic art from Renaissance art, "whether it is a pictorial or a plastic, an epic or a dramatic representation."[8] Boiardo's art is Gothic to the extent that it is episodic (and paratactic, as suggested earlier.) As Hauser says:

> The basic form of Gothic art is juxtaposition. ...Gothic art leads the onlooker from one detail to another and causes him, as has been well said, to 'unravel' the sucessive parts of the work one after the other; the art of the Renaissance, on the other hand, does not allow him to linger on any detail to separate any single element from the whole composition, but forces him rather to grasp all the parts at one and the same time.[9]

Unlike Boiardo, Ariosto is concerned with the total effect of his art. It is with the principle of unity in mind that Ariosto reminds

---

[8] Arnold Hauser, *The Social History of Art*, Vol. II: *Renaissance, Baroque, Mannerism* (New York: Random House, n. d.), p. 10. My intention is not to suggest that the *Innamorato* does not have a place in the body of Renaissance literature. I wish rather to point to its transitional nature, which reflects some decidedly Gothic aesthetic standards (as defined by Panofsky, Frey, Hauser, *et. al.*), and a medieval cosmological orientation. My view of the poem as the representation of a world coming into being rather than as a microcosm which exists *in facto*, like the *Furioso* or *Finnegan's Wake*, is supported by the conclusion of Antonio Franceschetti that "il Boiardo concepiva il suo poema in una forma di narrazione 'aperta' (p. 291, "Struttura e incompiutezza dell'*Orlando innamorato*," in *Il Boiardo e la critica contemporanea*, cited above, Introduction, note 18)." It remains, in other words, for Ariosto to ascend to the level of *poeta velut alter deus*, in the words of Scaligero. On the question of Late Gothic elements in the *Innamorato*, see Georg Weise, "Elementi tardogotici nella letteratura italiana del Quattrocento," (cited above, Chapter One, note 35), and Aldo Scaglione, "The Question of Naturalism in Late Medieval and Early Renaissance Art," in *Nature and Love in the Late Middle Ages* (Berkeley and Los Angeles, 1963), 221-223. While Professor Scaglione finds Weise's "alliance of naturalism and Late Gothic...all but meaningless in the literary field," he does allow that "One can fairly easily go along with the interpretation of the Italian chivalric genre (especially in the case of the *Orlando Innamorato*) in the light of Late Gothic taste and inspiration (p. 228)." It is undoubtedly true that the term Gothic has not always been applied judiciously to literary productions. Strictures against the use of Gothic in describing one medieval poet's works are found in Peter E. Bondanella, "The Theory of the Gothic Lyric and the Case of Bernart de Ventadorn," paper read at the MLA annual meeting, Chicago, 1971. The most comprehensive discussion of the Gothic in literature is found in Paul Frankl, *The Gothic* (Princeton, 1960).

[9] *Ibid.*, pp. 10-11

his audience that he has complete control over the design of his weave. Like the painters named by Hauser (Masaccio, Donatello, Andrea del Castagno, and others), Ariosto strives "...despite all the fullness of detail and colour, to make a total impression." [10]

In Boiardo's poem the stress on the present moment and on the individual character leads to both synchronic and diachronic discontinuity. The faulty memory of the Poet (to which he admits) and his inability to see beyond the horizon of immediate events completely dampens what harmony (i.e., "simultaneously apperceived polyphony" [11]) might exist between the dominant episode and whatever action may be occurring elsewhere, beyond the immediate range of perception of poet and audience. Thus when Orlando goes off in pursuit of Angelica he simply ceases to be a defender of Charlemagne's kingdom; and when he is battling monsters he is totally devoted to the delights of combat and ceases to be a lover in pursuit of a lady.

As Ariosto weaves the various threads of his *textum*, however, he creates a tapestry which remains permanently before us until the last thread is tied and Rodomonte's soul falls to the shores of Acheron. Even when a thread is abandoned it remains a "living" part of the whole picture as, for example, when the Poet leaves Ruggiero swimming in the ocean:

> Ma mi parria, Signor, far troppo fallo,
> se, per voler di costor dir, lasciassi
> tanto Ruggier nel mar, che v'affogassi. [12]
> (XLI.46)

It is of course a joke, but we are nonetheless invited to believe that Ruggiero continues to exist and struggle until he is rescued. Likewise, Olimpia will continue to suffer (X.35) until the Poet-Creator rescues her. They are threads hanging over the scene of an incomplete tapestry. In the end we will have a totality which shows a multiplicity of actions occurring simultaneously.

In Boiardo's Poem, however, the various episodes are like frames in a motion picture film; there is movement in that part which

---

[10] *Ibid.*, p. 10.
[11] Spitzer, p. 44.
[12] All citations of Ariosto are to *Orlando furioso*, ed. Santorre DeBenedetti and Cesare Segre (Bologna, 1960).

is projected before the audience, but it is quickly lost in the circling reel of static moments. Thus when Brandimarte finds Agricane's body (II.19.28) thirty-one cantos after the King's death, the corpse is uncorrupted, as if he had been dead only three hours:

> Parlava in questo modo il cavalliero
> A quel re morto con piatoso core,
> Il quale era ancor bello e tutto intiero,
> Sì come occiso fosse di tre ore.

Here as elsewhere whatever is not part of the present moment simply does not exist. There is no *continuum*, no *durée* which effects transformations. Time exists only as action; Doing is the only form of Being which has any place in this poetic world. Ariosto's construct differs, for, if Time does not exist as a unifying principle, it is replaced by Space, so that the various "threads" possess "some kind of existence before being combined into the weave." [10] They only need to be properly positioned by the demiurge. But when Boiardo's characters leave the stage of the present moment they lose their existence only to be reborn as if from nowhere, at a later moment, as is Pirandello's Madama Pace.

Boiardo's characters have been described as mechanical beings,[13] like puppets, which they are, off stage. On stage, however, they do come to life, and if the Poet does not portray their cerebral life, it is because they are not rational beings, but emotional beings existing with no need to question their existence. They are perfectly adapted to the world in which they live. Unlike tragic heroes these epic heroes need not prepare the way to action with the metaphysical anguish of auto-analysis. If they are automatons it is because they *can* respond immediately, instinctively, to any situation, for they exist in an "univers dans lequel les réponses sont présentés avant que ne soit formulées les questions." [14] It is a world in which all behavior is as absurd, as irrational, as that of Angelica after drinking from the fountain

---

[13] Zottoli, *Dal Boiardo all'Ariosto*, p. 76.
[14] Lucien Goldman, "Introduction aux premiers écrits de Georges Lukacs," in Lukacs' *Théorie du Roman*, cited above, p. 171.

of Love. There is neither history nor predictability in this world; the life of the characters is as discontinuous as the life of the natural cycle. Spring, we are told, is more delightful for coming after Winter, but Winter does not exist in the Poem. All action occurs in Spring, in April, May or June.

Just as the *Innamorato* is a collection of detached moments, thereby differing from Ariosto's more unified world, so also do the spatial concepts of the two poets differ. As a consequence each has a different geographical orientation. Boiardo's analysis of the poetic world is simply topographic, while Ariosto's is truly geographic if not cosmographic. Ariosto's world is seen from a distance so great that details are obscured; at the same time, however, the whole is more strikingly unified. While his contemporary, Magellan, is circling the globe by sea, Ariosto assigns Ruggiero the task of circling the globe by air:

>   Quindi partì Ruggier, ma non rivenne
>   per quella via che fe' già suo mal grado
>   allor che sempre l'ippogrifo il tenne
>   sopra il mare, e terren vide di rado:
>   ma potendogli or far batter le penne
>   di qua di là, dove più gli era a grado,
>   volse al ritorno far nuovo sentiero,
>   come, schivando Erode, i Magi fèro.
>
>   Al venir quivi, era, lasciando Spagna
>   venuto India a trovar per dritta riga,
>   là dove il mar oriental la bagna;
>   dove una fata avea con l'altra briga.
>   Or veder si dispose altra compagna,
>   che quella dove i venti Eolo instiga,
>   e finir tutto il cominciato tondo,
>   per aver, come il sol, girato il mondo.
>   (X.69-70)

Ariosto's stage is the Earth itself reduced, through the power of the hippogriff, to a "global village". Boiardo, by contrast to Ariosto, is less interested in real geography.[15] Even the Forest of

---

[15] For a discussion of Boiardo's use of real geography see Santino Caramella, "L'Asia nell'Orlando Innamorato," *Bollettino della Società Geografica Italiana*, Series 5, 3 (1923), Fasc. i-ii, 44-49; Fasc. iii-iv, 127-150.

Ardenne, the site of the founts of Love and Hate, is not accurately located in the *Innamorato*. Not only is it not located where the *real Bois d'Ardenne* is to be found, but its location even changes within the poem itself. Boiardo is more interested in the topographical description of the illusory world of enchanted gardens and their inhabitants. Never is he more accurate, for example, than when he describes Falerina's Garden in Orgagna, which disappears when Orlando cuts down a tree in the center which bears golden apples (II.5.4-15). The garden, which took seven months to create (II.5.17), is described as being thirty miles in circumference and surrounded by a stone wall "mille braccie" high (II.4.16). It has four entrances, each guarded by a ferocious monster. There is a marble entrance on the east side guarded by a dragon, a silver gate on the north defended by a giant, a west entrance defended by a donkey with a razor-sharp tail, and to the south a gate guarded by a bull with horns of fire and iron. Between Canto Seventeen of Book One, where the Garden is first described, and Cantos Four and Five of Book Two, where it is entered and destroyed by Orlando, the Poet, who relies heavily on his memory, forgets none of the details of its description.

Boiardo's characters never see the horizon as Ariosto's Ruggiero does; they only see topographical landmarks such as a red cliff (I.5.59), ominous rivers and bridges, a cave, crossroads, fountains in forests, towers of imprisonment, enchanted palaces above and below ground, and all the monsters and maidens that populate a world of fantasy. The Poet may not know where the *selva di Ardena* is, but he knows where the *Fiume del Riso* is, he knows that the *Ponte della Rose* (II.2.41) was once called *Ponte Periglioso*, and, of course, he notices every patch of red and white flowers along the road to that bridge.

Boiardo's world, as we have said, is infinite because of its infinite divisibility, and it is eternal because of the lack of consciousness of time. There is no awareness of time as the limited personal asset it is to the bourgeois consciousness,[16] which Ariosto's characters perhaps reflect to some extent by insisting on their fair share of time on the stage of their microcosmic existence:

---

[16] Cf. von Martin, pp. 15-16.

> Di questo altrove io vo' rendervi conto;
> ch'ad un gran duca è forza ch'io riguardi,
> il qual mi grida, e di lontano accenna,
> e priega ch'io nol lasci ne la penna.
>
> (XV.9)

The world as Boiardo's Poet sees it is an inexhaustible natural world made for man to enjoy is every detail, for as Orlando tells Agricane, it was made by God expressly for mankind:

> — Questo che or vediamo, è un bel lavoro,
> Che fece la divina monarchia;
> E la luna de argento, e stelle d'oro,
> E la luce del giorno, e li sol lucente,
> Dio tutto ha fatto per la umana gente. —
>
> (I.18.41)

It is a world which is as natural as it is fantastic; it is a balance between the natural-seeming imaginary world of a fanciful poet and the marvelous-seeming natural world of a country nobleman. All of Boiardo's similes, for example, offset the fantastic elements in the Poem by employing images of common wildlife, simple vegetation and ordinary natural phenomena: leaves, ice, straw and fire, flowers, wind, spiders, flies, butterflies, wasps, pheasants, falcons, dogs, wild boar, cabbage, mushrooms, the sea and an occasional *leone* or *serpente*. A later Italian literature will combine the perspectives of Boiardo and Ariosto, as does Bruno, for example, or Marino, who views the world from Ariosto's distant vantage point, but through a telescope, thereby preserving the details of close-range observation.

BIBLIOGRAPHY

Allodoli, Ettore. "Grandezza e novità del Boiardo," *Rinascita*, 3 (February, 1940), 3-70.
Anceschi, Giuseppe, ed. *Il Boiardo e la critica contemporanea. Atti del convegno di studi su Matteo Maria Boiardo, Scandiano-Reggio Emilia 25-27 Aprile 1969.* Florence: Leo S. Olschki, 1970.
Andreas Capellanus. *The Art of Courtly Love.* Translated by John Jay Parry. New York, 1964.
Ariosto, L. *Orlando furioso.* Edited by Santorre DeBenedetti and Cesare Segre. Bologna, 1960.
Aristotle. *De anima.* Translated by Kenelm Foster and Silvester Humphries. New Haven, 1954.
Arthos, John. *On the Poetry of Spencer and the Form of Romance.* London, 1956.
Azzolina, Liborio. *Il mondo cavalleresco in Bojardo, Ariosto, Berni.* Palermo, 1912.
Bertoni, Giulio. *La biblioteca estense e la coltura ferrarese ai tempi del Duca Ercole I (1471-1505),* Torino, 1903.
———. *L'Orlando furioso e la rinascenza a Ferrara.* Modena, 1919.
———. *Nuovi studi su Matteo Maria Boiardo.* Bologna, 1904.
Bigi, Emilio. *La poesia del Boiardo.* Florence, 1941.
Boccaccio, G. *Il Decameron.* Edited by Charles S. Singleton. Bari, 1955.
Boiardo, Matteo Maria. *Opere volgari: Amorum libri, Pastorale, Lettere.* Edited by Pier Vincenzo Mengaldo. Bari, 1962.
———. *Orlando Innamorato, Amorum Libri.* Edited by Aldo Scaglione. 2 vols. Torino, 1966.
———. *Tutte le opere.* Edited by Angelandrea Zottoli. 2 vols. Milan, 1944.
Bonadeo, Alfredo. "Note sulla pazzia di Orlando," *Forum Italicum,* 4 (1970), 39-57.
Bonfatti, Alfredo. "Il fiabesco nel Boiardo," *Humanitas,* 3 (1948), 489-495.
Bosco, Umberto. *La lirica del Boiardo.* Rome, 1964.
Bronzini, Giovanni B. *Tradizione di stile aedico dai cantari al 'furioso'.* Florence, 1966.
Caramella, Santino. "L'Asia nell'Orlando Innamorato," *Bollettino della Società Geografica Italiana,* Series 5, 3 (1923), Fasc. i-ii, 44-49; Fasc. iii-iv, 127-150.
Carrara, Enrico. *I due Orlandi.* Torino, 1935.
Cassirer, Ernst. *The Individual and the Cosmos in Renaissance Philosophy.* Translated by Mario Domandi. New York and Evanston, 1963.

Castiglione, Baldesar. *The Book of the Courtier.* Translated by Charles Singleton. New York, 1959.
Catalano, Michele, ed. *La Spagna.* 3 vols. Bologna, 1939-40.
Chimenz, Siro A. *La rappresentazione dell'amore nel poema del Bojardo.* Rome, 1931.
Contini, Gianfranco, ed. *Poeti del Duecento.* 2 vols. Milan, 1960.
Croce, Benedetto. *Ariosto, Shakespeare e Corneille.* Bari, 1920.
———. *La letteratura italiana per saggi.* Vol. I. Bari, 1956.
———. *Poeti e scrittori del pieno e del tardo rinascimento.* Vol. II. Bari, 1945. Vol. III. Bari, 1952.
Curtius, Ernst Robert. *European Literature and the Latin Middle Ages.* Translated by Willard R. Trask. New York, 1953.
Dante. *Il convivio.* Edited by G. Busnelli and G. Vandelli. 2 vols. Florence, 1964.
———. *La vita nuova.* Edited by Michele Barbi. Florence, 1932.
De Robertis, Domenico. "L'esperienza poetica del Quattrocento." *Storia della letteratura italiana.* Vol. III. Milan: Garzanti, 1966.
De Sanctis, Francesco. *La poesia cavalleresca e scritti vari.* Edited by Mario Petrini. Bari, 1954.
———. "Storia della letteratura italiana." *Opere.* Edited by Niccolò Gallo. Milan, 1961.
Durling, Robert M. *The Figure of the Poet in Renaissance Epic.* Cambridge, Massachusetts, 1965.
Edwards, Ernest W. *The Orlando Furioso and its Predecessor.* Cambridge, England, 1924.
Ferrari, G.; Campanini, N.; Rajna, P.; Luzio, A.; and others. *Studi su Matteo Maria Boiardo.* Bologna, 1894.
Foffano, Francesco. *Il poema cavalleresco.* Milan, 1905.
Foscolo, Ugo. *Opere edite e postume.* Vol. IV: *Prose letterarie.* Florence, 1939.
———. *Opere edite e postume.* Vol. X: *Saggi di critica storico-letteraria.* Florence, 1859.
Franceschetti, Antonio. "La 'Spagna in rima' e il duello di Orlando e Agricane," *Lettere Italiane,* 21 (1969), No. 3, 322-326.
———. "Struttura e incompiutezza dell'*Orlando innamorato*," in *Il Boiardo e la critica contemporanea. Atti del convegno di studi su M. M. Boiardo.* Edited by Giuseppe Anceschi. Florence: Leo S. Olschki, 1970. 281-294.
Frankl, Paul. *The Gothic.* Princeton, 1960.
Gardner, Edmund G. *Dukes and Poets in Ferrara.* London, 1904.
———. *The King of Court Poets: A Study of the Work and Life of Lodovico Ariosto.* New York, 1968.
Garin, Eugenio. *Il rinascimento italiano.* Milan, 1941.
———. "Motivi della cultura filosofica ferrarese nel rinascimento." *La cultura del rinascimento italiano.* Florence, 1961.
Goldmann, Lucien. "Introduction aux Premiers Écrits de Georges Lukacs," *Temps Modernes,* No. 195, August, 1962, 254-280.
Goldthwaite, Richard A. *Private Wealth in Renaissance Florence, A Study of Four Families.* Princeton, 1968.
Gostoli, Giancarlo. "L'unità dell'ispirazione lirica nella poesia di Matteo Maria Boiardo," *Letterature Moderne,* 9 (1959), 437-456.
Griffiths, E. T. ed. *Li Chantari di Lancellotto.* Oxford, 1924.

Hauser, Arnold. *The Social History of Art*. Vol. II: *Renaissance, Mannerism, Baroque*. Translated by Stanley Godman. New York: Random House, n.d.
Hauvette, Henri. *L'Arioste et la Poésie Chevaleresque à Ferrare au Début du XVIe Siècle*. Paris, 1927.
Hegel, G. W. F. *The Philosophy of Fine Art*. Translated by F. P. B. Osmaston. Vol. II. London, 1920.
Hill, R. T. and Bergin, T. G., eds. *Anthology of Provençal Troubadours*. New Haven, 1957.
Lacan, Jacques. *The Language of the Self; The Function of Language in Psychoanalysis*. Translated with notes and commentary by Anthony Wilden. Baltimore, 1968.
Lukacs, Georges. *La Théorie du Roman*. Translated by Jean Clairevoye. Geneva, 1963.
Luzio, A. and Renier, R. "La cultura e le relazioni letterarie di Isabella d'Este Gonzaga," *Giornale Storico della Letteratura Italiana*, 35 (1900), 193-257; 42 (1903), 75-111.
Malvasi, Giuseppe. *La materia poetica del ciclo brettone in Italia*. Bologna, 1903.
Marinelli, Peter Vincent. "The Dynastic Romance: a Study in the Evolution of the Romantic Epics of Boiardo, Ariosto and Spencer." Unpublished Ph.D. dissertation, Princeton University, 1964.
Martin, Alfred von. *Sociology of the Renaissance*. New York and Evanston, 1963.
Mengaldo, Pier Vincenzo. *La lingua del Boiardo lirico*. Florence, 1963.
Panzini, Alfredo. *Matteo Maria Boiardo*. Messina, 1918.
Pettinelli, Rosanna Alhaique. "L'Orlando Innamorato e la tradizione cavalleresca in ottave: I. Raffronti di personaggi e situazioni." *Rassegna della Letteratura Italiana*. Series 7, 71 (1967), 383-418.
Pico della Mirandola. "Oration on the Dignity of Man." *The Renaissance Philolosophy of Man*. Edited by E. Cassirer, P. O. Kristeller and J. H. Randall, Jr. Chicago, 1948.
Piemontese, Filippo. *La formazione del Canzoniere boiardesco*. Milan, 1953.
Ponte, Giovanni. "Le fontane d'Ardenna dell'Orlando innamorato," *Giornale Storico della Letteratura Italiana*, 129 (1952), 383-392.
―――. "Matteo Maria Boiardo." *I classici italiani nella storia della critica*. Edited by Walter Binni. Vol. I. Florence, 1965.
Pound, Ezra. *Literary Essays*. New York, 1968.
Procacci, Virgilio. *La vita e l'opera di Matteo Maria Boiardo*. Florence, 1931.
Rajna, Pio. *Le fonti dell'Orlando furioso*. Florence, 1900.
Reichenbach, Giulio. *L'Orlando innamorato di M. M. Boiardo*. Florence, 1936.
―――. *Matteo Maria Boiardo*. Bologna, 1929.
―――. "Matteo Maria Boiardo." *Orientamenti culturali: i minori*. Vol. I. Milan, 1961.
Rho. Edmondo. *Primitivi e romantici*. Florence, 1937.
Ridolfi, Roberto. *Vita di Girolamo Savonarola*. 2 vols. Rome, 1952.
Ross, W. D. *Aristotle*. New York, 1963.
Rossi, Vittorio. *Il Quattrocento*. Milan, 1933.
Rougemont, Denis de. *Love in the Western World*. Translated by Montgomery Belgion. New York, 1957.

Saccone, Eduardo. "Note ariostesche," *Annali della Scuola Normale Superiore di Pisa,* Series 2, 28 (1959), 193-242.

———. "Osservazioni su alcuni luoghi dell'*Innamorato*," MLN, 86 (1971), 31-60.

Salutati, Coluccio. *De nobilitate legum et medicinae, De verecundia.* Edited and translated by Eugenio Garin. Florence, 1947.

Scaglione, Aldo. "Chivalric and Idyllic Poetry in the Italian Renaissance," *Italica,* 33 (1956), 252-260.

———. "Matteo Maria Boiardo," *Grande Dizionario Enciclopedico.* Vol. III. Torino, 1957, 231-234.

———. *Nature and Love in the Late Middle Ages.* Berkeley and Los Angeles, 1963.

Schevill, Ferdinand. *The Medici.* New York, 1960.

Searles, Colbert. "The Leodilla Episode in Bojardo's Orlando Innamorato," *Modern Language Notes,* 17, No. 7 (November, 1902), p. 205, column 410.

Shearman, John. *Mannerism.* Baltimore, 1967.

Singleton, Charles S. *An Essay on the Vita Nuova.* Cambridge, Massachusetts, 1958.

Spitzer, Leo. *Classical and Christian Ideas of World Harmony.* Edited by Anna Granville Hatcher. Baltimore, 1963.

Symonds, John Addington. *Renaissance in Italy: Italian Literature.* 2 vols. London and New York, 1904.

Tenerani, Luciano "L'Orlando Innamorato: appunti per la lettura dei primi due canti," *Ausonia,* 20 (1965), 37-43.

Ugolini, Francesco A. *I cantari d'argomento classico.* Florence, 1933.

Valency, Maurice. *In Praise of Love.* New York, 1958

Visconti, Alessandro. *La storia dell'Università di Ferrara (1391-1950).* Bologna, 1950.

Voigt, F. T. A. *Roland-Orlando dans l'Épopée Française et Italienne.* Leiden, 1938.

Weise, Georg. "Elementi tardogotici nella letteratura italiana del Quattrocento," *Rivista di Letterature Moderne e Comparate,* 10 (1957), 101-199.

Wilkins, E. H. "The Naming of Rodamonte," *Modern Language Notes,* 70, 596-599.

Zitarosa, G. R. "Il Boiardo," *Aspetti Letterari,* 5 (1965), 1-21.

Zottoli, Angelandrea. *Dal Boiardo all'Ariosto.* Milan, 1934.

———. *Di Matteo Maria Boiardo, discorso.* Florence, 1937.

www.ingramcontent.com/pod-product-compliance
Lightning Source LLC
Chambersburg PA
CBHW020421230426
43663CB00007BA/1265